Close-Up
English in Use

STUDENT'S BOOK

B1+

Philip James

Australia • Brazil • Japan • Korea • Mexico • Singapore • Spain • United Kingdom • United States

Contents

Unit	Grammar	Vocabulary
1 pages 4–8	present simple; present continuous; stative verbs	collocations & expressions; exam practice; writing
2 pages 9-13	the indefinite article: *a/an*; the definite article: *the*	collocations & expressions; exam practice; writing
3 pages 14-18	past simple; past continuous;	phrasal verbs; exam practice; writing
4 pages 19-23	*used to* & *would*; *be used to* & *get used to*;	word formation; exam practice; writing
Review 1 pages 24-27	Grammar Exam practice: cloze, open cloze, Grammar & Vocabulary	
5 pages 28-32	present perfect simple; present perfect continuous	prepositions; exam practice; writing
6 pages 33-37	countable nouns; uncountable nouns; quantifiers	collocations & expressions; exam practice; writing
7 pages 38-42	future simple; *be going to*; future continuous; future perfect simple;	word formation; exam practice; writing
8 pages 43-46	temporals	phrasal verbs; exam practice; writing
Review 2 pages 47-50	Grammar Exam practice: word formation, cloze, Grammar & Vocabulary	
9 pages 51-55	*can* & *could*; *may* & *might*; *must*; *should*; *would*; *needn't*; *be able to*; *have to*; *mustn't* & *don't have to*	prepositions; exam practice; writing
10 pages 56-60	*may/might have*; *should have*; *could have*; *can't/couldn't have*; *must have*; *would have*; *needn't have*	collocations & expressions; exam practice; writing
11 pages 61-65	past perfect simple; past perfect continuous	phrasal verbs; exam practice; writing
12 pages 66-70	question tags; reflexive pronouns; indefinite pronouns; possessive pronouns	word formation; exam practice; writing
Review 3 pages 71-74	Grammar Exam practice: open cloze, word formation, Grammar & Vocabulary	

Unit	Grammar	Vocabulary
13 pages 75-79	gerunds, infinitives; full infinitives; bare infinitives; gerund or infinitive?	collocations & expressions; exam practice; writing
14 pages 80-84	comparison of adjectives & adverbs; other comparative structures; *too*, *enough*, *so* & *such*;	prepositions; exam practice; writing
15 pages 85-89	passive voice: tenses; passive voice: gerunds, infinitives & modal verbs	phrasal verbs; exam practice; writing
16 pages 90-93	passive voice: impersonal & personal structures	word formation; exam practice; writing
Review 4 pages 94-97	Grammar Exam practice: cloze, open cloze, Grammar & Vocabulary	
17 pages 98-103	reported speech: statements; reported speech: changes in time & place; reported speech: questions	collocations & expressions; exam practice; writing
18 pages 104-108	reported speech commands & requests; reported speech: reporting verbs	prepositions; exam practice; writing
19 pages 109-113	zero conditional; first conditional; second conditional; third conditional; mixed conditionals	word formation; exam practice; writing
20 pages 114-117	conditionals without *if*; *wish* & *if only*	phrasal verbs; exam practice; writing
Review 5 pages 118-121	Grammar Exam practice: word formation, cloze, Grammar & Vocabulary	
21 pages 122-125	relative clauses; defining relative clauses; non-defining relative clauses	collocations & expressions; exam practice; writing
22 pages 126-129	participle clauses	prepositions; exam practice; writing
23 pages 130-133	causative	phrasal verbs; exam practice; writing
24 pages 134-137	inversion: *under no circumstances*, *never* & *not only ... but also*; *it's (about/high) time*	word formation; exam practice; writing
Review 6 pages 138-141	Grammar Exam practice: open cloze, word formation, Grammar & Vocabulary	

Irregular verbs 142 **Collocations & Expressions** 146
Phrasal verbs 144 **Word formation** 147
Prepositions 145

Unit 1

Awareness

1 Which of these sentences are correct (C) and incorrect (I)?

1. Jenny live in a big house. ___
2. We usually work on Saturday mornings. ___
3. What colour is Tom paint his bedroom? ___
4. The kids are danceing in the garden. ___
5. I once a week go to the gym. ___
6. Are you coming to dinner tonight? ___
7. I don't watch often TV. ___
8. Why is she always asking you for money? ___
9. No, I not going out tomorrow night. ___
10. We're having a party next weekend. ___

How many did you get right? ☐

Grammar

Present Simple

Affirmative	Negative	Questions
I/we/you/they play he/she/it plays	I/we/you/they **don't** play he/she/it **doesn't** play	**Do** I/we/you/they **play**? **Does** he/she/it **play**?
Short Answers		
Yes, I/we/you/they **do**. **Yes**, he/she/it **does**.	**No**, I/we/you/they **don't**. **No**, he/she/it **doesn't**.	

We use the Present Simple for
- facts or general truths.
*Apples **grow** on apple trees.*
- routines or habits (often with adverbs of frequency).
*I **often wear** a hat in the summer.*
- permanent states.
*Maria **lives** in a big flat in Madrid.*
- timetabled events in the future.
*Our train **arrives** at 7.45 tomorrow morning.*

> **Note**
> Some common time expressions that are often used with the Present Simple are *every day/week/month/summer, every other day, once a week, twice a month, at the weekend, in January, in the morning/afternoon/evening, at night, on Tuesdays, on Friday mornings*, etc.
> *They go to the south of France **every summer**.*

Remember! We often use adverbs of frequency with the Present Simple. They tell us how often something happens. They come before the main verb, but after the verb *be*.
*Tom **rarely** uses the Internet.*
*We **always** watch TV in the evenings.*

Some common adverbs of frequency are: *always* (most often), *usually, sometimes, rarely / hardly ever / seldom, never* (least often)

Present Continuous

Affirmative	Negative	Questions
I **am** ('**m**) play**ing** he/she/it **is** ('**s**) play**ing** we/you/they **are** ('**re**) play**ing**	I **am** ('**m**) **not** play**ing** he/she/it **is not** (**isn't**) play**ing** we/you/they **are not** (**aren't**) play**ing**	**Am** I play**ing**? **Is** he/she/it play**ing**? **Are** we/you/they play**ing**?
Short Answers		
Yes, I **am**. **Yes**, he/she/it **is**. **Yes**, we/you/they **are**.	**No**, I'**m not**. **No**, he/she/it **isn't**. **No**, we/you/they **aren't**.	

Spelling: dance → danc**ing**, travel → travel**ling**, tidy → ti**dying**

4

We use the Present Continuous for
- actions that are in progress at or around the time of speaking.
I'm **doing** my homework.
- actions that are temporary.
Simon **is staying** with his aunt at the moment.
- situations that are changing or developing in the present.
Exams **are getting** more difficult.
- an annoying habit (often with *always, continually, constantly* and *forever*).
You **are always trying** to play tricks on me.
- narratives (eg as story, a joke, a plot, and sports commentaries)
A man **is sitting** in the park. He **is reading** a newspaper. Suddenly ...
- what is happening in a picture.
Some people **are lying** on the beach. A child **is playing** with her dog.
- plans and arrangements for the future.
They **are going** on holiday next month.

> **Note**
> Some common time expressions that are often used with the Present Continuous are *at the moment, now, for the time being, this morning/afternoon/evening/week/month/year, today*, etc.
> I'm sleeping on the sofa **for the time being**.

Stative Verbs

Some verbs are not usually used in continuous tenses. They are called stative because they describe states and not actions. To talk about the present, we use these verbs in the Present Simple tense. The most common of these are:
- verbs of emotion: *hate, like, love, need, prefer, want.*
I **hate** the colour brown.
- verbs of senses: *feel, hear, see, smell, sound, taste.*
This coffee **smells** great.
- verbs which express a state of mind: *believe, doubt, forget, imagine, know, remember, seem, suppose, think, understand.*
I **imagine** she lives in a beautiful house.
- verbs of possession: *belong to, have, own, possess.*
My uncle **owns** this shop.
- other verbs: *be, consist, contain, cost, include, mean.*
How much does this jacket **cost**?

Some verbs can be both stative verbs and action verbs, but with a different meaning. The most common of these verbs are:

be	Sam **is** very well behaved. (usual behaviour) He's **being** very naughty just now. (at the moment; not their normal behaviour)
expect	I **expect** she is very pleased with her results. (expect = think or believe) We're **expecting** rain this weekend. (expect = wait for)
have	Susan **has** five brothers. (have = own/possess) They're **having** a fantastic time at summer camp. (have = experience)
look	She **looks** like a film star. (look like = resembles) I'm **looking** for a new laptop. (look for = search)
taste	This milk **tastes** bad. (taste = have a particular flavour) The chef **is tasting** the soup. (taste = test the flavour)
think	He **thinks** he's a great singer. (think = have an opinion) They're **thinking** of selling their car. (think = consider)
see	I **see** what you mean now! (see = understand) I'm **seeing** the doctor this afternoon. (see = meet)
smell	Dinner **smells** delicious! (smell = have a particular smell) Why **are** you **smelling** your socks? (smell = action of smelling)
weigh	Dan **weighs** 52 kg. (weigh = have a particular weight) The butcher **is weighing** the mince. (weigh = measure the weight)

Unit 1

Grammar Exercises

2 Circle the correct words.
1. Wendy always **reads / is reading** the back page of the newspaper first.
2. My parents **have / are having** dinner at an expensive restaurant tonight.
3. I **don't watch / 'm not watching** romantic films.
4. We **go / are going** to the theatre once a month.
5. Greg **stays / is staying** in bed for the time being.
6. I hardly ever **wear / am wearing** shoes in the house.
7. How **do you get / are you getting** to school every day?
8. Can you be quiet please? I **try / am trying** to do some work.
9. What **do you do / are you doing** at the moment?
10. **Does she come / Is she coming** out with us on Friday?

3 Complete the sentences with the correct form of the Present Simple or the Present Continuous of the verbs in brackets.
1. The children _____ (play) in the front room at the moment.
2. I _____ (have) dinner at my friend's house tomorrow evening.
3. Light _____ (travel) at 186,000 miles per second.
4. Mr James _____ (teach) us maths on Wednesdays.
5. She _____ (always / try) to get better marks than me at school. It's so annoying!
6. We _____ (go) to Italy every winter.
7. The last performance _____ (start) at eleven o'clock.
8. I _____ (not eat) anything at the moment because I _____ (feel) ill.

4 Choose the correct time expression to complete the sentences.
1. Sandra is working on her project ___.
   a usually
   b now
   c hardly ever
2. We spend a lot of time at the beach ___.
   a every summer
   b this summer
   c next summer
3. I ___ have time to practise the guitar.
   a this morning
   b once a week
   c rarely
4. Why are you ___ arguing with me?
   a always
   b today
   c seldom
5. Sorry, madam. We don't have any tomato soup ___.
   a never
   b every day
   c this evening
6. The Barkers are going camping ___.
   a next weekend
   b constantly
   c twice a month

5 Match the questions with the answers.
1. What are you drinking at the moment? ☐
2. Is your dad an accountant? ☐
3. Do your grandparents live in a big flat? ☐
4. Is it a beautiful day today? ☐
5. How often do you go swimming? ☐
6. Are the children sleeping on the floor? ☐
7. Does your uncle drive a taxi? ☐
8. Are you worrying about the exams? ☐
9. Where are you going on holiday this year? ☐
10. Do I have ink on my face? ☐

a Tea.
b No, I'm not.
c Yes, you do.
d No, he isn't.
e Yes, it is.
f Every week.
g Yes, they are.
h No, they don't.
i Yes, he does.
j The USA.

6 Complete the sentences with the correct form of the Present Simple or Present Continuous of the verbs in bold.

1 **expect**
 a I _____ you'll be hungry by the time you get home tonight.
 b We _____ a letter from the head teacher this week.
2 **have**
 a Your car _____ a flat tyre.
 b Where _____ (we) lunch this afternoon?
3 **think**
 a Izzy _____ of going to cookery classes.
 b What _____ (you) of the latest Marvel comic movie?
4 **see**
 a She _____ her boyfriend at seven o'clock this evening.
 b I hope you _____ what I mean now.
5 **weigh**
 a How much _____ (the baby)?
 b I _____ myself at the moment because I think I've put on weight.

7 Write questions using the correct form of the verbs.

1 you / eat / in a restaurant / every week?
 Do you eat in a restaurant every week?
2 what time / John / usually / come home?
 _____
3 how many instruments / Mark / play?
 _____
4 you / do / your homework at the moment?
 _____
5 why / the little girl / cry?
 _____
6 who / you / usually / go / to the cinema with?
 _____
7 she / think / of moving to a new house?
 _____
8 why / you / smell / the milk?
 _____

Vocabulary

Collocations & Expressions

8 Match the expressions with their meanings.

1 save time ☐
2 make a difference ☐
3 keep in touch ☐
4 break the ice ☐
5 save your strength ☐
6 make trouble ☐
7 break a habit ☐
8 keep your promise ☐

a to continue to communicate with someone
b to do what you said you were going to do
c to relax, so as not to waste energy
d to do something that prevents wasting time
e to make people relax in a social situation
f to stop doing something that you used to do often
g to deliberately cause problems
h to have a positive effect

Unit 1

9 Complete the sentences with these words.

> black blue gold green pink red

1 I love babysitting for the Barkers because the children are as good as _____.
2 She was _____ with envy when she saw her sister's beautiful new dress.
3 Our teacher saw _____ when nobody in the class could answer the question.
4 I'm tickled _____ that you enjoyed that cake I made for you.
5 When he's feeling _____, he likes to go to the cinema to cheer himself up.
6 Daniel is the _____ sheep of the family – he's the only one who didn't go to university.

Exam Practice

10 Complete the second sentence so that it has a similar meaning to the first sentence, using the word given. Do not change the word given. You must use between two and five words.

1 Simon really resembles his father.
   like
   Simon really _____ his father.

2 My brother complains about my music all the time.
   continually
   My brother is _____ about my music.

3 We seldom go camping without our dog.
   often
   We _____ without our dog.

4 I go to karate classes every Wednesday and Friday with my cousin.
   twice
   I go to karate classes _____ with my cousin.

5 Jake nearly always stays in bed until after 8 am.
   hardly
   Jake _____ before 8 am.

6 My new bike is very light.
   weigh
   My new bike _____ very much.

7 The departure time of our flight is 22.45.
   at
   Our flight _____ 22.45.

8 We have an appointment to see the head teacher this afternoon.
   are
   We _____ this afternoon.

11 Use the word in capitals to form a word that fits in the gap.

1 Why didn't you invite her to the party? That wasn't very _____. **THOUGHT**
2 Pauline needed to take a month off work because she was suffering from _____. **DEPRESS**
3 You should ask David to do it if it's important – he's _____. **TRUST**
4 The government says the new laws will help to improve economic _____. **STABLE**
5 She's a very popular and _____ woman. **ATTRACT**
6 We love going to our villa in the countryside – it's so quiet and _____. **PEACE**
7 A lot of _____ have moved into the neighbourhood recently. **FOREIGN**
8 He's funny, and he has a great _____, but he doesn't have enough qualifications for the job. **PERSON**

Writing

12 Write a paragraph in your notebook. Describe what you are wearing today. Then write what you usually wear at the weekend.

Unit 2

Awareness

1 Which of these sentences are correct (C) and incorrect (I)?

1. Mr Stevens is doctor. ___
2. I'll see you in an hour. ___
3. The sun is bright today! ___
4. We took a trip down Thames in the London. ___
5. I'm learning to play the piano. ___
6. Do you speak the French? ___
7. My dad is great songwriter. ___
8. You're the funniest person I know. ___
9. Have you ever been to the Australia? ___
10. He travelled the world by motorcycle. ___

How many did you get right? ☐

Grammar

The Indefinite Article: A/An

We use *a* before a consonant sound.
a professor   *a* university
We use *an* before a vowel sound.
an accountant   *an* hour   *an* MP3 player

We use *a/an*
• with singular countable nouns.
*Jake is **a** chemist.*
• to mean per/each in expressions of frequency.
*I used to go swimming three times **a** week.*
• to mention something for the first time. (When we continue talking about it we use *the*.)
*I've got **a** new bike. **The** bike has 18 gears.*
• to show job, status, etc.
*She's **a** famous actress.*

The Definite Article: The

We use *the* with singular and plural countable nouns and uncountable nouns to talk about something specific when the noun is mentioned for a second time.
*At last, there's **a** bus! Oh no, **the** bus isn't stopping.*

We also use *the* before
• unique nouns.
***The** moon looks bigger when it's near the horizon.*
• names of cinemas, theatres, ships, hotels, etc.
*We're going to **the** Rialto Theatre tonight.*
*How much is a room in **the** Grand Hotel?*
• names of rivers, deserts, mountain ranges, and names or nouns with *of*.
*Where are **the** Himalayas?*
*Have you seen **the** Tower of Pisa?*
• countries or groups of countries whose names are plural.
*She was born in **the** Philippines.*
*We went to **the** United States last year.*
• musical instruments.
*Do you play **the** violin?*
• nationalities.
***The** Brazilians love their football.*

Unit 2

- adjectives used as nouns.
*It's only fair to tax **the** rich more than **the** poor.*
- superlatives.
*He's **the** fastest sprinter in school.*
- these words: *beach, countryside, station, jungle,* etc.
*How long would you survive in **the** jungle?*
- *morning, afternoon, evening.*
*I hate getting up in **the** morning.*

We do not use *the* before
- proper nouns.
*Dave is in **Spain**.*
- subjects of study.
*Do you prefer **English** or **Geography**?*
- names of countries, cities, streets (BUT: *the High Street*), squares, bridges (BUT: *the Golden Gate Bridge*), parks, stations, individual mountains, islands, lakes, continents.
*Paris is the capital of **France**.*
*I'll meet you on **Spencer Road**, opposite **Lakeview Park**.*
- *bed, church, school, hospital, prison, university, college, court* when we talk about something related to the main purpose of the place. (Work never takes *the*.)
*Graham is in **hospital**.* (He is ill.)
*Graham's mum has gone to **the** hospital to visit him.* (Graham's mum is not ill; she's gone to see Graham)
- means of transportation in expressions like *by car*, etc. (BUT: in *the* car).
*We travelled **by train**.*
- names of *sports, games, colours, days, months, drinks, holidays, meals,* and *languages* (not followed by the word language).
*My sister's football **team** wears **blue**.*
*What did you eat for **lunch** on **Saturday**?*

> **Note**
> When we refer specifically to a meal, a colour, a drink, etc then we use *the*.
> ***The breakfast** at the hotel was terrible.*
> ***The tea** you made was very nice, thank you.*

Grammar Exercises

2 Circle the correct words.

1 I have a driving lesson once **the / a / –** week.
2 It's dangerous to go swimming when **the / a / –** sea is so rough.
3 She toured Europe by **the / a / –** train last summer.
4 Uncle Sam is **the / an / –** expert rock climber.
5 I hope Greece wins **the / a / –** World Cup.
6 Oh, no! We've got **the / a / –** biology this afternoon.
7 He's always tired when he gets home from **the / a / –** work in **the / an / –** evening.
8 There's **the / a / –** new café on **the / a / –** High Street.

3 Complete the sentences with *the* or no article (–).

1 Have you ever seen _____ Eiffel Tower?
2 I forgot to eat _____ breakfast this morning!
3 I think I left my keys in _____ car.
4 Stan's cousin is in _____ prison for burglary.
5 She moved to _____ countryside when she retired.
6 We didn't enjoy _____ soup last night, but _____ dessert was delicious.
7 What's _____ best present you've ever had for _____ Christmas?
8 The kids are playing _____ basketball in _____ garden.

4 Complete the sentences with **the**, **a**, **an** or **no article (–)** where necessary.

1. Have you read _____ book I lent you?
2. There was _____ strange light in _____ sky last night.
3. She's studying in _____ Germany, but she doesn't speak _____ German.
4. Only Mark made _____ useful contribution to _____ discussion.
5. Is _____ golf _____ easy sport to master?
6. Some people think _____ life of _____ teacher is _____ easy one.
7. Nearly everyone believes that _____ peace is preferable to _____ war.
8. When I was at _____ school, my favourite subject was _____ geography because I enjoyed learning about continents like _____ Asia.

5 Complete the dialogue with **the**, **a**, **an** or **no article (–)** where necessary.

Sam: It was my birthday on **(1)** _____ Sunday.
Julie: Did you have **(2)** _____ party?
Sam: No, **(3)** _____ party was cancelled.
Julie: That's **(4)** _____ pity. Was it cancelled because of **(5)** _____ weather?
Sam: Yes. I wanted **(6)** _____ barbecue in **(7)** _____ garden, but it was too rainy.
Julie: I hope you had **(8)** _____ fun anyway. What presents did you get?
Sam: I got **(9)** _____ bike and **(10)** _____ electric guitar.
Julie: I didn't know you played **(11)** _____ guitar.
Sam: I don't. I'm starting **(12)** _____ lessons next week at **(13)** _____ music school next to **(14)** _____ Manor Park.
Julie: That's a long way from **(15)** _____ home, isn't it?
Sam: Yes, it is. That's what **(16)** _____ new bike is for.

6 Complete the text with **the**, **a**, **an** or **no article (–)** where necessary.

Hi Elaine,

How are you feeling? It's **(1)** _____ shame you missed **(2)** _____ school today because it was **(3)** _____ most interesting day of **(4)** _____ year so far! We have **(5)** _____ new student in our class. His name is Mark and he's from **(6)** _____ USA. **(7)** _____ teacher told me to look after him and show him around **(8)** _____ school! He's **(9)** _____ really nice person. We had **(10)** _____ lunch together in the canteen and he told me all about **(11)** _____ life in **(12)** _____ America.

Mark's dad is **(13)** _____ accountant, which is funny because Mark hates **(14)** _____ maths! In fact, he prefers **(15)** _____ sport to any other school subject. He told me he was **(16)** _____ best tennis player in his school – and he's only 13. I asked him if he was good at **(17)** _____ football, and he said yes – but then we realised we were talking about **(18)** _____ different game! **(19)** _____ Americans call it **(20)** '_____ soccer' – and he doesn't like that game at all.

Get well soon,
Maria.

Unit 2

7 Find the mistakes and correct the sentences.

1 I've got a great news for you.

2 Amazon is a very long river.

3 Do you speak the Portuguese?

4 What are we having for the dinner?

5 Greta is going to the college next year.

6 This is an unique opportunity for me.

7 Greg is rich businessman.

8 I never learned to play a piano.

9 We went to the top of an Empire State Building in New York.

10 What did you have for the breakfast?

Vocabulary

Collocations & Expressions

8 Complete the phrases with these prepositions. You will need to use some prepositions more than once.

| at | in | of | on | to | with |

1 shout _____
2 have confidence _____
3 have an effect _____
4 rely _____
5 be associated _____
6 be engaged _____
7 be involved _____
8 approve _____

9 Complete the sentences with the correct form of the phrases from 8.

1 My mother doesn't want me to _____ our neighbour's children anymore, because they're always getting into trouble.
2 The film had a very strong _____ me – I couldn't stop thinking about it for days.
3 The government has complete _____ its plan to improve living conditions in the city.
4 Stan has just become _____ Susan – they're getting married in the spring.
5 You can _____ me to help you whenever you need me.
6 Her parents don't _____ her new boyfriend. They think he's a bad person.
7 We're starting a new film project for the art club – would you like to _____ it?
8 Please don't _____ me – I can hear you perfectly clearly when you talk in a normal voice.

12

Exam Practice

10 Complete the second sentence so that it has a similar meaning to the first sentence, using the word given. Do not change the word given. You must use between two and five words.

1. Steve has gone to Italy to learn the language.
   Italian
   Steve is _____ Italy.

2. I want to have a positive effect on the world.
   make
   I want to _____ in the world.

3. Sonia was delighted when I gave her the flowers.
   pink
   Sonia _____ when I gave her the flowers.

4. My aunt teaches engineering at the local college.
   teacher
   My aunt _____ at the local college.

5. We went to dance classes on Mondays and Wednesdays when we were children.
   twice
   We went to dance classes _____ when we were children.

6. Danny is a really good guitarist.
   guitar
   Danny _____ well.

7. Nobody in our school swims faster than me.
   fastest
   I _____ in our school.

8. The basketball team my brother plays for has a red strip.
   wears
   My brother's _____ red.

11 Use the word in capitals to form a word that fits in the gap.

1. Sarah is successful because she has a lot of _____. **CONFIDENT**
2. Too much _____ is bad for a relationship. **JEALOUS**
3. There's a _____ man hanging around outside the building. **SUSPECT**
4. I used to be very good at _____ when I was younger. **GYMNAST**
5. How many times has your team won the _____? **CHAMPION**
6. He's fun to be with because he's always so _____. **CHEER**
7. Some people are _____ good at sports. **NATURE**
8. The government needs to spend more money on _____. **EDUCATE**

Writing

12 In your notebook, make a list of places near your home which
- you would recommend to a visitor.
- you don't have, but would like.

Use *the* and *a/an*.

I recommend **the** café on Bloom Street.
We don't have **a** museum.

Unit 2 13

Unit 3

Awareness

1 Which of these sentences are correct (C) and incorrect (I)?

1. I read a lot of books last year. ___
2. We didn't walked home. ___
3. She got up early on the morning. ___
4. They were watching TV at eight o'clock. ___
5. The dog didn't wanting a bath. ___
6. He was riding a horse when he felled. ___
7. Were you studying all day? ___
8. Did all the students passed the test? ___
9. They didn't go out last night. ___
10. I wasn't feeling well that morning. ___

How many did you get right? ☐

Grammar

Past Simple

Affirmative	Negative	Questions
I/he/she/it/we/you/they work**ed**	I/he/she/it/we/you/they **didn't** work	**Did** I/he/she/it/we/you/they **work**?
Short Answers		
Yes, I/he/she/it/we/you/they **did**.	No, I/he/she/it/we/you/they **didn't**.	

Spelling: dance → danc**ed**, travel → trave**lled**, stu**dy** → stu**died**, stay → stay**ed**

We use the Past Simple for
• something that started and finished in the past.
*He **studied** French at university.*
• past routines and habits (often with adverbs of frequency).
*Katy **often climbed** trees when she was little.*
• actions that happened one after the other in the past, for example when telling a story.
*The burglar **went** upstairs and **entered** the main bedroom.*

Note
Some verbs are irregular and do not follow these spelling rules. See a list of irregular verbs on pages 142–143.

Note
Some common time expressions that are often used with the Past Simple are *yesterday, last night/week/month/summer, a week/month/year ago, twice a week, once a month, at the weekend, in March, in the morning/afternoon/evening, at night, on Thursdays, on Monday mornings*, etc.
*I watched a film about World War 2 **last night**.*

Past Continuous

Affirmative	Negative	Questions
I/he/she/it **was** work**ing** we/you/they **were** work**ing**	I/he/she/it **was not (wasn't)** work**ing** we/you/they **were not (weren't)** work**ing**	**Was** I/he/she/it work**ing**? **Were** we/you/they work**ing**?
Short Answers		
Yes, I/he/she/it **was**. **Yes**, we/you/they **were**.	**No**, I/he/she/it **wasn't**. **No**, we/you/they **weren't**.	

Spelling: write → writ**ing**, travel → trave**lling**, stu**dy** → stu**dying**

We use the Past Continuous for
• actions that were in progress at a specific time in the past.
*We **were playing** chess at nine o'clock last night.*
• two or more actions that were in progress at the same time in the past.
*I **was reading** while the baby **was sleeping**.*
• giving background information in a story.
*The sun **was shining** hotly and people **were sitting** around in the shade.*
• an action that was in progress in the past that was interrupted by another action.
*Mary **was running** down the stairs when she **tripped** and hurt herself.*

Note

Some common time expressions that are often used with the Past Continuous are *while, as, all day/week/month/year, at ten o'clock last night, last Sunday/week/year, this morning*, etc.
*They were playing cricket on the beach **all afternoon**.*

Grammar Exercises

2 Circle the correct words.

1 I **walked / was walking** the dog when it started to rain.
2 **Did / Were** you see that shooting star?
3 That **wasn't / wasn't being** a very funny joke.
4 The audience **clapped / was clapping** when the performance ended.
5 **Did you work / Were you working** when the teacher came in the room?
6 How many children **did you take / were you taking** to the park yesterday?
7 **We didn't get / Weren't getting** any tickets because they were too expensive.
8 He **went / was going** downstairs and **ran / was running** out of the door.
9 While I **slept / was sleeping** a bird **flew / was flying** through the window.
10 It **rained / was raining** when I **left / was leaving** school this afternoon.

3 Complete the sentences with the correct form of the Past Simple or Past Continuous of the verbs in brackets.

1 We _____ (discover) a new café in the city last night.
2 Sammy _____ (tidy) his room when his mum _____ (come) in.
3 They _____ (go) to the library and _____ (borrow) a book about Peru.
4 I _____ (text) while the teacher _____ (talk).
5 Martha _____ (hear) a noise outside her tent, so she _____ (shout) for help.
6 _____ (you / see) the programme about the Aztecs last night?
7 What book _____ (John / read) when you _____ (meet) him?
8 She _____ (hurt) herself while she _____ (decorate) the garage.

Unit 3   15

Unit 3

4 Match the questions with the answers.

1. Were you sleeping?
2. Did your sister enjoy the film?
3. Where did they stay?
4. Were those boys bothering you?
5. Was it raining when you got home?
6. What did David say to you?
7. Did those people pay for their tickets?
8. Did you finish your homework?
9. Why was she crying?
10. Who told you my secret?

a. No, I didn't.
b. Because she was sad.
c. Yes, I was.
d. Yes, it was.
e. No, they didn't.
f. In a hotel.
g. Yes, she did.
h. No, they weren't.
i. Daniel.
j. Nothing.

5 Complete the dialogue with the correct form of the Past Simple or Past Continuous of the verbs in brackets.

Mia: Hey, Steve. You'll never guess what I (1) _____ (see) last night.
Steve: What (2) _____ (you / see)?
Mia: A UFO! I (3) _____ (wake) up at about two in the morning, and I (4) _____ (not can) get back to sleep. So I (5) _____ (go) downstairs for some milk.
Steve: What (6) _____ (happen) then?
Mia: I (7) _____ (pour) the milk into a glass when I (8) _____ (hear) a strange noise outside.
Steve: What (9) _____ (you / do) next?
Mia: I (10) _____ (open) the back door, and (11) _____ (look) up into the sky. A large white light (12) _____ (float) above the trees! Then suddenly it (13) _____ (fly) up into the sky and (14) _____ (disappear) behind the clouds.
Steve: (15) _____ (your mum or dad / see) it too?
Mia: No, they (16) _____ (sleep).
Steve: I don't believe you. I think you (17) _____ (dream).
Mia: I (18) _____ (not dream). It (19) _____ (be) real!

6 Complete the questions to the answers.

1. A: _____ at seven o'clock yesterday morning?
   B: No, I wasn't having breakfast. I was still in bed!
2. A: What time _____?
   B: I got up at 8.30.
3. A: _____ when you went outside?
   B: No, the sun wasn't shining. It was raining.
4. A: Why _____ yesterday afternoon?
   B: I went to the library because I needed a quiet place to study.
5. A: _____ anyone there?
   B: Yes, I met my friend Jake.
6. A: What _____?
   B: He was wearing jeans and a T-shirt.
7. A: _____ when he came into the library?
   B: Yes, I was studying.
8. A: _____ anywhere interesting after the library?
   B: No, we didn't. We both went home.

7 Complete the sentences with the word that best fits each gap.

1 I _____ working on a project about the Incas last night.
2 _____ you remember to take a photo?
3 Tim was painting his room _____ he fell off the ladder.
4 We ate dinner at six o'clock _____ the evening.
5 _____ the twins playing nicely together when you got home?
6 How long _____ they waiting for?
7 **A:** Was it a good show?
   B: No, it _____.
8 What time _____ you finally arrive?

Vocabulary

Phrasal verbs

8 Match the phrasal verbs with their meanings.

1	believe in	a	to remain on the same topic
2	let out	b	to make a certain sound
3	look into	c	to happen
4	make out	d	to manage to see something which is difficult to see
5	make up	e	to trick or deceive somebody
6	take in	f	to examine or study something
7	take place	g	to think that something exists
8	stick to	h	to say something that isn't true

9 Complete the sentences with the correct form of the phrasal verbs in 8.

1 I don't believe your UFO story. I think you _____ it _____.
2 The old lady was completely _____ by the robber's story.
3 If you look closely at the painting, you can just _____ the name of the artist.
4 I wish our teacher would _____ one topic – he keeps changing the subject!
5 She _____ a terrible scream when she saw what was behind the door.
6 I used to _____ ghosts, but I don't anymore.
7 My dad promised to _____ the possibility of buying me a motorbike.
8 The ghost hunt will _____ tomorrow evening at 10 pm.

Unit 3

Exam Practice

10 Complete the second sentence so that it has a similar meaning to the first sentence, using the word given. Do not change the word given. You must use between two and five words.

1 We had our end-of-term party in the gym.
   took
   Our end-of-term party _____ the gym.

2 During our walk in the woods, we saw a UFO.
   were
   We _____ when we saw a UFO.

3 I don't think that vampires exist.
   in
   I don't _____ vampires.

4 When we got near to the lion, it roared.
   let
   The lion _____ roar when we got near to it.

5 When I called, Tom was still asleep.
   sleeping
   Tom _____ I called.

6 After starting the engine, Sally drove away.
   then
   Sally _____ drove away.

7 I was reading and my sister was watching a DVD at the same time.
   while
   My sister _____ I was reading.

8 Mike spent last summer reading books about crop circles.
   lot
   Mike _____ of books about crop circles last summer.

11 Use the word in capitals to form a word that fits in the gap.

1 If a place is _____, that means that there are too many people living there. **POPULATE**
2 The first people to arrive lived in a _____ near the coast. **SETTLE**
3 The police are looking into the _____ of a 60-year-old woman – we hope they'll find her soon. **APPEAR**
4 Your muscles will _____ if you don't exercise them regularly. **WEAK**
5 There will be an _____ into this tragic accident. **INVESTIGATE**
6 I woke up to see a _____ light shining in the sky. **MYSTERY**
7 My brother wants to be an _____ when he finishes university. **ARCHAEOLOGY**
8 Arthur was a _____ king of England. **LEGEND**

Writing

12 Write a paragraph in your notebook. Write about what you and your family were doing at eight o'clock last night. What did you do after that?

Unit 4

Awareness

1 Which of these sentences are correct (C) and incorrect (I)?

1. I used to play a lot of tennis. ___
2. He would love swimming when he was a child. ___
3. Did you use to live in France? ___
4. They would take the dogs to the forest every weekend. ___
5. I'm not used to my new bike yet. ___
6. You'll get used to it soon. ___
7. Mark didn't use to like carrots. ___
8. I was used to getting up early very quickly. ___
9. She thought she would never used to her new shoes. ___
10. We use to study computer science at our old school. ___

How many did you get right? ☐

Grammar
Used to & Would

We use *used to* + bare infinitive for
• actions that we did regularly in the past, but that we don't do now.
*My sister **used to play** the violin when she was young.*
• states that existed in the past, but that don't exist now.
*Paul **used to prefer** walking everywhere, but now he always rides his scooter.*

We use *would* + bare infinitive for actions that we did regularly in the past, but that we don't do now. We don't use it for past states.
*We **would go** to the beach every day when we lived in Australia.*

Be Used To & Get Used To

We use *be used to* + gerund/noun to talk about something that is usual or familiar.
*Fred **is used to working hard** because he was brought up on a farm.*

We use *get used to* + gerund/noun to talk about the process of something becoming familiar.
*I'm slowly **getting used to the idea** of having my own flat.*

Note
Be and *get* change depending on the tense that is needed in the context.
*She's **used to fixing** engines. She's had lots of experience.*
*Andrea **has been getting used to** her new mobile phone.*

Grammar Exercises

2 Circle the correct words.

1. When I was a baby I **used to / would** love bananas and chocolate sauce.
2. She isn't used to **work / working** so hard.
3. We would **eat / eating** fish for dinner every Friday evening.
4. These walls **used to / would** be yellow.
5. They **would / were used to** send me £10 every birthday.
6. Don't worry, you'll soon **be / get** used to sleeping in a tent.
7. I **would / used to** understand Portuguese, but I can't anymore.
8. He **wouldn't / wasn't used to** stay up after ten o'clock when he was a boy.
9. She isn't nervous because she **is used to / gets used to** giving speeches.
10. It took me a long time to **be / get** used to doing so much homework.

Unit 4

3 How did people live 200 years ago? Complete the sentences with **used to** or **didn't use to**.

1 They _____ travel by plane.
2 They _____ travel by horse.
3 They _____ write emails.
4 They _____ write letters.
5 Children _____ work in factories.
6 They _____ live as long as we do.
7 They _____ have telephones.
8 They _____ have cleaner air than we have now.

4 Write the questions to the answers in this interview with an old person.

1 where / play?
  Where did you use to play?
  I used to play in the street with my friends.
2 how / get to school?
  _____
  I used to walk.
3 have / lots of friends?
  _____
  Yes, I did.
4 go abroad on holiday?
  _____
  No, I never went abroad.
5 your dad / have a car?
  _____
  Yes, he did.
6 enjoy / school?
  _____
  No, I never liked it.
7 what subject / be good at?
  _____
  I used to be good at maths.
8 get into trouble at school?
  _____
  No, I was a good boy!

5 Complete the sentences with the correct form of **be used to** or **get used to**.

1 I (not) _____ working on Sundays.
2 She says she'll never _____ driving such a big car.
3 We _____ getting lots of homework at this school.
4 My friends (not) _____ seeing me with short hair.
5 It was hard at first, but I soon _____ it.
6 I don't mind having dinner late in the evening – I _____ it.
7 When she first arrived in England, she _____ taking an umbrella with her everywhere.
8 She soon _____ it!

6 Look at the situations and complete the sentences using **used to**.

1. You have to wear a uniform at your new school.
   You'll have to get used to wearing a uniform.
2. The Smiths moved from the country to the city. It's much noisier there.
   They weren't _____.
3. The children found life very different in the city, but it wasn't a problem for them.
   The children soon _____.
4. You usually go to bed before 10 pm, but last night you stayed up till midnight, so today you're very tired.
   You _____.
5. Sally has a new computer with a touch screen. She finds it difficult to use.
   She doesn't think she'll ever _____.
6. Tom lives in Ecuador. At first, he didn't like the hot weather, but he's okay with it now.
   Tom _____.

7 Complete the sentences with the word that best fits each gap.

1. We _____ to live in Brazil.
2. Did you _____ to like pop music?
3. When they were children, they _____ often climb the trees in their garden.
4. I'm not used _____ looking after animals.
5. She used to _____ a lot of tea, but now she prefers coffee.
6. He never _____ used to sharing a flat with two other people.
7. They hated it at first, but now they _____ used to it.
8. Mark couldn't finish his meal because he wasn't used to _____ so much.
9. How much money did you use _____ get for working in the café?
10. I didn't _____ to like cheese, but I love it now.

Vocabulary

Word formation

8 Complete the sentences with these words.

conclude   discover   explain   remark   reside   ridicule   similar   situate   stick   usual

1. When you _____ something, you find it for the first time.
2. The word _____ means to be or put in a particular place.
3. If you _____ something to something else, you join it with glue.
4. _____ means normal.
5. If you _____ somewhere, that's where you live.
6. To _____ means to decide something after studying or thinking about it.
7. Something _____ to another thing is nearly the same as it.
8. When you make a _____, you say your opinion about something.
9. You _____ something when you make it easy to understand and give information about it.
10. If you _____ something or someone you make fun of them, and try to make others laugh at them.

Unit 4

9 Use the word in capitals to form a word that fits in the gap.

1 Nobody understood the teacher's _____. — **EXPLAIN**
2 That was a very _____ football match. — **REMARK**
3 It's _____ for it to rain so much in the summer – something strange is happening to our climate. — **USUAL**
4 All the _____ of the tower block had to leave the building when the fire alarm went off. — **RESIDE**
5 That's the most _____ thing I've ever heard! — **RIDICULE**
6 We found ourselves in a very difficult _____ when we couldn't afford to pay our electricity bill. — **SITUATE**
7 Scientists have made an interesting _____ this month. — **DISCOVER**
8 What's that _____ stuff on the sofa? Is it chocolate? — **STICK**
9 I can see the _____ between you and your father. — **SIMILAR**
10 We finally came to the _____ that it was not a good idea to go camping that weekend. — **CONCLUDE**

Exam Practice

10 Complete the second sentence so that it has a similar meaning to the first sentence, using the word given. Do not change the word given. You must use between two and five words.

1 On Friday evenings, we usually went to a restaurant in town.
   used
   On Friday evenings, _____ to a restaurant in town.

2 It didn't take long for the boys to adjust to their new life.
   got
   The boys _____ their new life.

3 Every time we went to the beach, our dog stole someone's ice cream.
   would
   Our dog _____ every time we went to the beach.

4 It was difficult for her to walk in high heels at first, but now it's easy.
   is
   Now _____ in high heels.

5 This club wasn't so popular last year.
   be
   This club _____ so popular last year.

6 Would you check under your bed for monsters when you were a child?
   to
   When you were a child, _____ under your bed for monsters?

7 I never enjoyed going to the theatre, but I do now.
   use
   I _____ going to the theatre.

8 Wearing glasses won't bother you after a few days.
   get
   You'll _____ glasses after a few days.

11 Choose the correct answers.

1 I __ to love riding my skateboard when I was a boy.
 a would b used c use
2 It will take a while to __ used to the busy roads here.
 a get b have c be
3 Every day during the summer we __ take the bus to the seaside.
 a would b used c use
4 Did you __ to enjoy playing in the woods?
 a would b used c use
5 He hates it because he __ not used to it yet.
 a is b would c gets
6 How long did it take you to get used to __ your phone?
 a use b using c used
7 We didn't use to __ much homework in primary school.
 a getting b got c get
8 __ Sonia used to walking to work every day?
 a Is b Does c Has

Writing

12 Write a paragraph in your notebook. Write about what you used to do/think/believe when you were six years old.

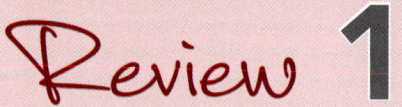 

Grammar

1 Complete the sentences with the correct form of the Present Simple or Present Continuous of the verbs in brackets.

1 The kids _____ (watch) a film about penguins.
2 _____ (you / think) about grandpa? Don't worry, I'm sure he'll be fine.
3 How much _____ (the baby / weigh)?
4 I _____ (take) guitar lessons this summer.
5 Our train _____ (leave) at 9.35.
6 Mmm – this fish _____ (taste) great!
7 Why _____ (you / be) so silly now?
8 Simon _____ (not look) like his father.
9 I _____ (not stay) at my friend's house tonight.
10 _____ (your dog / enjoy) swimming in the sea?

2 Complete the sentences with a/an, the or no article (–).

1 She always goes to school by _____ bus.
2 I hate Monday mornings – we've got _____ maths from 9 till 11.
3 That's _____ worst joke you've ever told me.
4 Martin goes swimming for _____ hour every morning.
5 Julia is _____ very good gymnast.
6 There's _____ new café on _____ Highfield Road.
7 We had _____ fantastic holiday in _____ Greece last year.
8 Did you go to _____ cinema in _____ evening?
9 They went to _____ hospital to visit _____ Maria.
10 She has to have _____ operation on _____ New Year's Day.

3 Complete the text with the correct form of the Past Simple or Past Continuous of the verbs in brackets.

I (1) _____ (work) on my computer last night when a message
(2) _____ (arrive) on my screen. It (3) _____ (be)
an email from an old friend. I (4) _____ (read) it, then
I (5) _____ (go) downstairs to tell my parents about it.
In the living room, my parents (6) _____ (watch) TV, and my sister
(7) _____ (read) a music magazine. 'What (8) _____
(happen)?' my mum (9) _____ (ask) me. 'You look happy.'
'I (10) _____ (get) an email from Tony,' I (11) _____ (say).
'What (12) _____ (he / say)?'
I (13) _____ (tell) them. 'Tony's coming to visit us this weekend.'
'Oh dear. We (14) _____ (not expect) any visitors this weekend! I'll have to go
shopping,' (15) _____ (reply) Mum.
When I (16) _____ (go) back upstairs, my mum
(17) _____ (write) a shopping list. She likes Tony. But my sister
(18) _____ (frown) – she doesn't like any of my friends!

4 Circle the correct words.

1 This park **used to / would** be much nicer.
2 When I was younger, I **didn't use to / wouldn't** enjoy dancing.
3 She **is / gets** used to working until past midnight.
4 Did it take you long to **be / get** used to living alone?
5 I **was used to / would** watch videos on the Internet in the evening.
6 What kind of car **did you use to / would you** drive?
7 Sue soon **was / got** used to her new job.
8 I hated living there because I **didn't get / wasn't** used to such cold weather.

5 Find the mistakes and correct the sentences.

1 I'm loving the colour blue.
   _____
2 These scissors doesn't work.
   _____
3 London is the capital of the England.
   _____
4 Dan is slowly being used to the new teacher.
   _____
5 We were running in the park when a dog was biting my leg.
   _____
6 Dave watched never TV.
   _____
7 I got the MP3 player for my birthday.
   _____
8 My parents would to drive me to school in the mornings.
   _____

6 Circle the correct words.

1 We**'re having / have** a party on Friday.
2 This coffee **is smelling / smells** delicious.
3 Did you enjoy **the / –** food they gave you?
4 I'm going to be **a / the** firefighter when I grow up.
5 Steve never **was / got** used to having a cat in the house.
6 What **did you do / were you doing** when the earthquake happened?
7 I used **to prefer / preferring** basketball to football.
8 John was reading **during / while** the kids were playing.

Review 1 25

Review 1

Exam Practice

7 For questions 1–12, read the text below and decide which answer (A, B, C or D) best fits each gap. There is an example at the beginning (0).

A spirit of adventure

Adventurers who (0) ___ in reaching their goal achieve fame and sometimes fortune. Those who fail have little to (1) ___ for their efforts.

A young man from England put aside a large part of his monthly (2) ___ for years so that he could cycle down the continent of South America. The (3) ___ that he chose meant that he would have to endure extremes, from the freezing cold of the Andes to the humidity of the Amazon jungle. His success (4) ___ on his plans working out perfectly.

It was a disaster. He was (5) ___ by mosquitoes, he almost drowned while crossing a river which had a much stronger (6) ___ than he had imagined, and he was arrested for not having official (7) ___ to cross a certain part of Peru. He was also (8) ___ for a variety of illnesses in several hospitals. He lost so much weight that he couldn't go on. Eventually he was found staggering along a (9) ___ mountain path. He soon (10) ___ out.

Back in Britain, he was interviewed at his (11) ___ hospital. When asked about his plans for the future, he answered with a (12) ___ grin that he would like to have another go.

0	A	manage	(B)	succeed	C	achieve	D	fulfil
1	A	show	B	exhibit	C	display	D	demonstrate
2	A	investment	B	salary	C	interest	D	money
3	A	way	B	route	C	track	D	course
4	A	trusted	B	stated	C	based	D	depended
5	A	stung	B	pecked	C	bitten	D	pinched
6	A	draught	B	drought	C	current	D	flood
7	A	permit	B	permission	C	allowance	D	pass
8	A	treated	B	cured	C	healed	D	recovered
9	A	remote	B	far	C	distant	D	solitary
10	A	went	B	passed	C	knocked	D	made
11	A	nearby	B	local	C	neighbourhood	D	country
12	A	long	B	extended	C	deep	D	broad

8 For questions 13–24, read the text below and think of the word which best fits each gap. Use only one word in each gap. There is an example at the beginning (0).

Rubber

Malaya is (0) ___the___ largest rubber producer in the world. Rubber is produced by making cuts in the bark of a rubber tree. When the bark (13) _____ cut, so are the tubes in the tree that carry a milky liquid containing rubber. The rubber is removed by adding a weak acid to (14) _____ milky liquid. A rubber tree can (15) _____ tapped for rubber when it is five years (16) _____ and it produces about three kilos of rubber a year.

The name 'rubber' reflects its first technical application. In 1771, it was used to rub (17) _____ pencil marks (18) _____ Joseph Priestly, the British chemist famous for his discovery of oxygen. In 1823, Charles Macintosh, a Scottish chemist (19) _____ name has been given to a type of coat, used rubber to (20) _____ cloth waterproof.

The most widely known process involving rubber is vulcanisation. In 1839, an American, Charles Goodyear, discovered this process, which is (21) _____ used today. Vulcanised rubber is quite different (22) _____ raw rubber because it becomes five times stronger during vulcanisation, in (23) _____ it is heated with sulphur and other ingredients to a temperature of about 150°C. Thousands of different articles in use today (24) _____ partly or wholly made of rubber.

Grammar

9 For questions 1–10, choose the word or phrase that best completes the sentence or conversation.

1. Sara wants to be ___ when she grows up.
   A the hairdresser
   B a hairdresser
   C an hairdresser
   D hairdresser

2. 'Have you got any plans for the weekend?'
   'We ___ a new computer!'
   A 're buying
   B buy
   C buying
   D to buy

3. 'I can't find it anywhere.'
   'What ___?'
   A do you look for
   B do you look like
   C are you looking for
   D are you looking like

4. 'Do you know any foreign languages?'
   'Yes, I ___ French lessons at school.'
   A would take
   B was taking
   C used to taking
   D took

5. 'Were you sleeping when I called?'
   'Yes, ___.'
   A I was
   B I wasn't
   C I did
   D I slept

6. We always ___ our uncle Matthew.
   A would enjoy visiting
   B enjoyed to visit
   C used to enjoy visiting
   D would enjoy to visit

7. I'm afraid we ___ a great time here in Manchester.
   A don't have
   B aren't having
   C not having
   D not have

8. What was Susan doing ___ you saw her?
   A while
   B as
   C where
   D when

9. I ___ like Tim, but I do now.
   A didn't use to
   B wasn't used to
   C wouldn't
   D didn't get used to

10. Did you go on holiday ___?
    A the last month
    B the month ago
    C last month
    D a last month

Vocabulary

10 For questions 11–20, choose the word or phrase that best completes the sentence or conversation.

11. I tried to help, but it didn't ___ any difference.
    A have
    B do
    C get
    D make

12. Sally was tickled ___ with her new MP3 player.
    A pink
    B blue
    C red
    D green

13. He has great confidence ___ his own abilities.
    A of
    B on
    C in
    D with

14. 'What does that sign say?'
    'I'm not sure. I can't ___ it out in this light.'
    A do
    B see
    C take
    D make

15. I was completely ___ in by his lies.
    A pushed
    B taken
    C held
    D given

16. Do you know a good way to ___ the ice at parties?
    A kill
    B smash
    C melt
    D break

17. I don't ___ of children playing games at the dinner table.
    A agree
    B approve
    C accept
    D admit

18. Don't listen to him – he's just trying to ___ trouble.
    A make
    B give
    C have
    D do

19. Martha ___ out a loud scream when she saw the black dog in her room.
    A took
    B let
    C stuck
    D got

20. Did the medicine have any ___ on you?
    A improvement
    B cure
    C situation
    D effect

Review 1 27

Unit 5

Awareness

1 Which of these sentences are correct (C) and incorrect (I)?

1 She has worked here for seven years. ___
2 You've won a fantastic prize just. ___
3 George has been ride his bike all afternoon. ___
4 Have you been crying? ___
5 Dan has been breaking his finger. ___
6 Where have they been hiding? ___
7 I've lived here since two months. ___
8 You haven't been concentrating. ___
9 We've been here twice so far. ___
10 He hasn't seen his grandmother for April. ___

How many did you get right? ☐

Grammar
Present Perfect Simple

Affirmative	Negative	Questions
I/we/you/they **have ('ve) seen** he/she/it **has ('s) seen**	I/we/you/they **have not (haven't) seen** he/she/it **has not (hasn't) seen**	**Have** I/we/you/they **seen**? **Has** he/she/it **seen**?
Short Answers		
Yes, I/we/you/they **have**. **Yes**, he/she/it **has**.	**No**, I/we/you/they **haven't**. **No**, he/she/it **hasn't**.	

Spelling: work → work**ed**, dance → danc**ed**, travel → travel**led**, study → stu**died**, play → play**ed**

We use the Present Perfect Simple for
• something that started in the past and has continued until now.
He**'s lived** in this flat for three years.
• something that happened in the past, but we don't know or we don't say exactly when.
The teacher **has spoken** to her parents.
• something that happened in the past and has a result that affects the present.
Steve **has lost** his laptop, so he can't finish his project.
• actions that have just finished.
I**'ve just heard** the news.
• experiences and achievements.
My brother **has won** lots of prizes for football.

Note
Some verbs are irregular and do not follow these spelling rules. See a list of irregular verbs and their past participles on pages 142–143.

Note
Some common time expressions that are often used with the Present Perfect Simple are *already, ever, for, for a long time, for ages, just, never, once, recently, since 2007/June, so far, twice, three times, until now, yet,* etc.
The film has **just** finished.

Remember! We use *have/has been* when someone has gone somewhere and has now returned, but we use *have/has gone* when someone has gone somewhere and is still there.
Simon **has been** to America. He showed us his photos last night.
Simon **has gone** to America. He will be back next week.

Present Perfect Continuous

Affirmative	Negative	Questions
I/we/you/they **have** (**'ve**) **been** keep**ing** he/she/it **has** (**'s**) **been** keep**ing**	I/we/you/they **have not** (**haven't**) **been** keep**ing** he/she/it **has not** (**hasn't**) **been** keep**ing**	**Have** I/we/you/they **been** keep**ing**? **Has** he/she/it **been** keep**ing**?
Short Answers		
Yes, I/we/you/they **have**. **Yes**, he/she/it **has**.	**No**, I/we/you/they **haven't**. **No**, he/she/it **hasn't**.	

Spelling: tak**e** → tak**ing**, run → run**ning**, stu**dy** → stu**dying**

We use the Present Perfect Continuous
• for actions that started in the past and are still in progress now or have happened repeatedly until now.
We **have been coming** to this same hotel for years.
• for actions that happened repeatedly in the past and have finished recently but that have results affecting the present.
The dog is wet because it**'s been swimming** in the river.
• to emphasise how long actions have been in progress for.
It**'s been raining** for six weeks!

Note

Some common time expressions that are often used with the Present Perfect Continuous are *all day/night/week, for years / a long time / ages, lately, recently, since*. We can use *How long ...?* with the Present Perfect Continuous in questions and *for (very) long* in questions and negative sentences.
She's been working on this project **for months**.

Grammar Exercises

2 Circle the correct words.

1 **Have you heard / Have you been hearing** the weather forecast?
2 The doctor **has given / has been giving** me a new prescription.
3 There you are! **Have you avoided / Have you been avoiding** me deliberately?
4 Rachel **has swum / has been swimming** – that's why her hair is wet.
5 Oh no! We **have missed / have been missing** the start of the show.
6 How long **have you tried / have you been trying** to phone me?
7 I **haven't seen / haven't been seeing** Julia for weeks.
8 We're tired because we **'ve done / 've been doing** aerobics.
9 He **'s visited / 's been visiting** the dentist twice this month.
10 Sorry I'm late. **Have you waited / Have you been waiting** for long?

3 Complete the sentences with **been** or **gone**.

1 **A:** Where's Tina?
   B: She's _____ shopping. She'll be back soon.
2 I've _____ shopping. Look what I bought!
3 We'd love to go to Australia. We've never _____ there.
4 The children aren't here. They've _____ to their grandparents' house.
5 Have you ever _____ to a hockey match?
6 Dad's _____ on a bike ride. I don't know when he'll be home.
7 Has Jack _____ to school already? He's left his bag on the table!
8 I don't have your medication because I haven't _____ to the chemist yet.

Unit 5

4 Complete the dialogue with the correct form of the Present Perfect Simple or Present Perfect Continuous of the verbs in brackets.

Jane: Oh, there you are Tim. I **(1)** _____ (look) for you all morning. Where **(2)** _____ (you / be)?

Tim: I **(3)** _____ (help) Sue fix her bike. It's really old. She **(4)** _____ (have) it for about five years now.

Jane: I know. I wonder why she **(5)** _____ (not ask) her parents to buy her a new one?

Tim: Her dad's business **(6)** _____ (not do) well for years, so they haven't got much money. Anyway – why **(7)** _____ (you / look) for me? What **(8)** _____ (happen)?

Jane: The back wheel **(9)** _____ (come) off my skateboard, and I don't know how to put it on again. Can you help?

Tim: Of course. I **(10)** _____ (fix) skateboards for years. I'm sure it won't be a problem!

Jane: You **(11)** _____ (do) a lot of fixing today!

Tim: I'm always happy to help.

5 Choose the correct answers.

1 Harry has been feeling ill ___ dinner time.
  a for
  b since
  c still

2 I ___ haven't heard from my new pen pal.
  a yet
  b lately
  c still

3 They haven't done their homework ___.
  a yet
  b for
  c still

4 Have you been given a spelling test ___?
  a still
  b lately
  c for

5 She's been in hospital ___ nearly two weeks.
  a for
  b lately
  c yet

6 Have you finished ___? That was quick!
  a already
  b yet
  c lately

6 Complete the questions.

1 **A:** <u>What medication have you been taking for your cold</u> ?
  B: I haven't been taking any medication for my cold.

2 **A:** How long _____?
  B: I've been going to aerobics classes for three months.

3 **A:** Where _____ my vitamins?
  B: I haven't put them anywhere! You had them in your hand a minute ago.

4 **A:** What _____ to your arm?
  B: I broke it when I was playing rugby.

5 **A:** Why _____?
  B: I've been avoiding fatty foods because I'm on a diet.

6 **A:** Where _____? I've been waiting for half an hour.
  B: I've been to the gym. Sorry.

7 **A:** _____ in the car again?
  B: Yes, the kids have been playing in the car all morning. Is it a mess?

8 **A:** What _____ today?
  B: I've done nothing! It's been a really lazy day.

30

7 Find the mistakes and correct the sentences where necessary. Put a tick (✓) below those which do not need correcting.

1 We've been using natural remedies since years.

2 This company has been selling herbal teas since 1881.

3 How many times have I been telling you not to eat so much meat?

4 Have you seen the doctor about your problem still?

5 Teresa has been forgetting her keys, so she can't open the front door.

6 Has he already left for the gym?

7 Samantha yet hasn't cleaned her room.

8 I haven't had any nourishing food for last month.

Vocabulary

Prepositions

8 Complete the phrases with these prepositions. You will need to use some prepositions more than once.

against   of   on   over   to

1 at risk _____
2 to work _____
3 to contribute _____
4 to focus _____
5 be a member _____
6 be vaccinated _____
7 live to be _____
8 to depend _____

9 Complete the sentences with the correct form of the phrases from 8.

1 Some cats can _____ 15 years old.
2 I can't come out because I need to _____ my geography project.
3 Mark doesn't know which university he is going to – it _____ his exam results.
4 When you concentrate on one thing, you _____ it.
5 If you don't wear a helmet when riding, you are _____ serious injury.
6 People sometimes use their cars unnecessarily, which _____ pollution in this city.
7 How long have you _____ this tennis club?
8 Children may suffer if they are not _____ diseases in early life.

Unit 5

Exam Practice

10 Complete the second sentence so that it has a similar meaning to the first sentence, using the word given. Do not change the word given. You must use between two and five words.

1. Mum is still cooking this evening's meal.
   not
   Mum _____ this evening's meal yet.

2. I started French lessons two years ago.
   learning
   I _____ two years.

3. Swimming all afternoon has made me feel very hungry.
   been
   I feel very hungry because _____ all afternoon.

4. She met Jake six months ago.
   known
   She _____ six months.

5. The Smiths are on holiday in Greece.
   to
   The Smiths _____ on holiday.

6. It's a long time since we have been to London.
   for
   We haven't _____ a long time.

7. He moved there in 2011 and he still lives there.
   living
   He _____ 2011.

8. It started raining four days ago, and it hasn't stopped yet.
   for
   It _____ four days.

11 Use the word in capitals to form a word that fits in the gap.

1. My cousin is training to be a _____. **DIET**
2. I went to the doctor and he _____ my injury. **EXAM**
3. Try to reduce your _____ of carbohydrates, and you might lose weight. **CONSUME**
4. Maria suffers from a rare _____ disease which means she has to take medicine every day. **GENE**
5. Children are under a lot of _____ to succeed in school these days. **PRESS**
6. Simon is so healthy – he has never had a serious _____ in his life. **ILL**
7. I'm sorry – I _____ rebooted your computer, and now you have lost your work. **ACCIDENT**
8. We like to go out and _____ with friends every Friday night. **SOCIAL**

Writing

12 Write five sentences in your notebook saying what you, your family, and your friends have NEVER done. Then write five more sentences saying what you have been doing, and for how long.

Unit 6

Awareness

1 Which of these sentences are correct (C) and incorrect (I)?

1 Welcome to the show, ladys and gentlemen. ___
2 There are some tomatoes in the fridge. ___
3 You have very white tooths. ___
4 Our research show that fruit is very healthy. ___
5 May I have a loaf of cheese, please? ___
6 Fresh food is good for you. ___
7 The news were very upsetting. ___
8 I'm sorry, your luggage is too heavy. ___
9 How much friends do you have? ___
10 There's a few milk left in the bottle. ___

How many did you get right? ☐

Grammar

Countable Nouns

Most nouns are countable and have singular and plural forms.

mechanic – mechanics
leaf – leaves
fish – fish
woman – women
foot – feet
lady – ladies
toy – toys
tomato – tomatoes

We usually use *a* or *an* with singular countable nouns.
a policeman
an operation

We can use *some*, *any* or a number (eg three) with plural countable nouns.
Here are **some** vitamins.
Are there **any** doctors?
He's been ill for **five** months.

We use singular or plural verb forms with countable nouns depending on whether we are talking about one or more items.
An orange **contains** a lot of vitamin C.
Oranges are good for you.

Remember! Some countable nouns don't end in -s. Remember to use a plural verb form with them.
Children are sometimes naughty.
Her **feet are** very small.

Uncountable Nouns

Some nouns are uncountable. They do not have plural forms.

advice	fruit	information	money	time
biology	fun	knowledge	music	traffic
cheese	furniture	luggage	progress	water
chocolate	health	medicine	research	weather
equipment	history	music	rubbish	
food	homework	milk	salt	

We don't use *a* or *an* with uncountable nouns. We can use *some* and *any*.
We need to buy **some** bread.
Have you got **any** news about Kevin?

We always use singular verb forms with uncountable nouns.
Fried food **is** not usually healthy.
Money **makes** the world go round.

Unit 6 33

Unit 6

> **Remember!** Some uncountable nouns end in -s. Remember to use a singular verb form with them.
>
> The news **is** very bad.
> Maths **is** my least favourite subject.
>
> We can use phrases describing quantity with uncountable nouns to say how much we have. The most common of these phrases are:
>
> - a bag of
> - a cup/glass of
> - a bottle of
> - a jar of
> - a bowl of
> - a loaf of
> - a can/tin of
> - a packet of
> - a carton of
> - a piece of
>
> I'd like **a glass of** water.
> There's **a bag of** crisps on the table.
>
> ## Quantifiers
>
> We use *some* with both uncountable and plural countable nouns in affirmative sentences and
> in requests or offers.
> Mum has made **some cupcakes**.
> Could I have **some milk**, please?
> Would you like **some help** with the cleaning?
>
> We use *any* with both uncountable and plural countable nouns in negative sentences and in questions.
> Susan doesn't want **any chocolate**.
> Are you inviting **any boys** to your party?
>
> We use *a lot of / lots of* with both uncountable and plural countable nouns.
> We eat **lots of cheese** in our house.
> Donna has got **a lot of fruit** in her bag.
>
> We use *a little* with uncountable nouns and *a few* with plural countable nouns in affirmative sentences.
> There's **a little money** left in my wallet.
> There are **a few students** who are ill today.
>
> We use *much* with uncountable nouns and *many* with plural countable nouns in negative sentences and in questions.
> How **much apple juice** do you want?
> There aren't **many gyms** which allow children.

Grammar Exercises

2 Complete the sentences using the plural form of the nouns in brackets.

1. Modern medicine has saved a lot of _____. (life)
2. The life expectancy for _____ in Okinawa is 78 years. (man)
3. Dentists recommend that you brush your _____ after every meal. (tooth)
4. It is important for _____ to get plenty of exercise. (child)
5. _____ can begin eating solid food at around five months of age. (baby)
6. We made a healthy salad with onions, cheese and some lettuce _____. (leaf)
7. How many _____ are in your aerobics class? (person)
8. Did you catch many _____ yesterday? (fish)
9. I drink five large _____ of water every day. (glass)
10. Can you buy some _____ when you are in town? (potato)

3 Are these nouns countable or uncountable? Put them in the correct row.

accident   brain   calorie   energy   health   herb   injection   milk   pain   soap   vitamin   weather

COUNTABLE	_____ _____ _____ _____ _____ _____
UNCOUNTABLE	_____ _____ _____ _____ _____ _____

4 Complete the sentences with **a**, **an**, **some** or **any**.
1. We need to buy _____ bandages.
2. Does _____ apple a day really keep the doctor away?
3. I'm sorry, I don't have _____ medicine to give you.
4. You need _____ of my homemade chicken soup.
5. Have you got _____ remedies for a headache?
6. There's _____ bowl of fruit in the kitchen – help yourself!
7. I need to make _____ appointment with my doctor.
8. Mum has _____ good news for you.
9. Please let us know if you have _____ allergies.
10. That's _____ painful looking injury!

5 Circle the correct words.
1. Don't forget to take a **bottle / bag** of water to the gym with you.
2. Can I have a **loaf / piece** of cheese, please?
3. There's a **carton / can** of milk in the fridge.
4. Every morning, I drink two **jars / cups** of tea.
5. We need a **loaf / packet** of bread.
6. How do you get through a whole **jar / glass** of honey every week?
7. One **piece / bowl** of cereal is all she eats in the morning.
8. Would you like a **can / piece** of lemonade?

6 Choose the correct answers.
1. I'm afraid we don't eat ___ of healthy food in our family.
   a much
   b a lot
   c many
2. Danny has ___ questions to ask the dietician.
   a a few
   b a little
   c a lot
3. Very ___ people take enough exercise.
   a much
   b little
   c few
4. Please may I have ___ money to buy a snack at break time?
   a a little
   b a lot
   c a few
5. There's ___ point in going on a diet if you don't stop smoking.
   a much
   b few
   c little
6. We don't have ___ time to do this project.
   a many
   b a lot
   c much
7. There are ___ things you can do to improve your health and fitness.
   a many
   b a lot
   c much
8. Always drink ___ of water when the weather is hot.
   a many
   b a few
   c lots

Unit 6 35

Unit 6

7 Write questions to the answers using **How much** or **How many**.

1 _____
  I've been to the gym three times this week.
2 _____
  There's about a litre of water in the bottle.
3 _____
  I've spent five pounds today.
4 _____
  I've been sitting here for two hours.
5 _____
  I need two cups of rice.
6 _____
  He's had a lot of experience.
7 _____
  I've been in hospital once.
8 _____
  She eats very little chocolate every day.

Vocabulary

Collocations & Expressions

8 Match the expressions with their meanings.

1 fresh as a daisy ☐
2 under the weather ☐
3 do you the world of good ☐
4 recharge your batteries ☐
5 pick someone's brains ☐
6 be back on your feet ☐
7 be on your last legs ☐
8 have a frog in your throat ☐

a to get your energy back
b to be extremely exhausted
c to recover from an illness which kept you in bed
d to feel slightly unwell
e to have difficulty speaking because you have a cough
f to feel well and awake
g to make you feel much better
h to ask an expert for information or advice

9 Complete the sentences with the correct form of the phrases from 8.

1 Martha, can I _____? I don't know anything about computers.
2 I don't usually sound like this when I talk – I _____.
3 She didn't feel great when she went to bed, but she woke up _____.
4 I really need a holiday to _____ after doing all those exams.
5 Jack has been working non-stop for nearly 24 hours, and now he's _____.
6 Drink this. It will _____.
7 I'm not really ill – I'm just feeling a bit _____, that's all.
8 After seven days in bed with the flu, Simon was _____ and playing football.

Exam Practice

10 Complete the second sentence so that it has a similar meaning to the first sentence, using the word given. Do not change the word given. You must use between two and five words.

1. You don't need to spend a lot of money to have a healthy diet.
   little
   You only need _____ to have a healthy diet.

2. I didn't go out because I wasn't feeling very well.
   weather
   I was _____, so I didn't go out.

3. There are very few gyms in this town.
   many
   There _____ gyms in this town.

4. You'll feel much better after a good night's sleep.
   world
   A good night's sleep will _____ good.

5. Three or four ideas mentioned at the meeting were silly.
   few
   There were _____ mentioned at the meeting.

6. We have very little food left in the house.
   much
   We _____ food left in the house.

7. He had to work really hard to get picked for the team.
   lot
   He had to do _____ to get picked for the team.

8. By the time she got home, she was absolutely exhausted.
   legs
   She was _____ by the time she got home.

11 Complete the sentences with the word that best fits each gap.

1. We haven't got _____ money in the bank.
2. You certainly eat a lot _____ vegetables, don't you?
3. I'm afraid the news _____ not good.
4. Can you get _____ carton of pineapple juice from the shop, please?
5. I take just a _____ sugar in my tea, thank you.
6. Harry has _____ allergy to cats.
7. How _____ times a week do you go swimming?
8. There's a little medicine left in the bottle, but not _____.

Writing

12 Write a paragraph in your notebook. Describe the contents of your fridge. Use some, any, a little, and a lot.

Unit 6 **37**

Unit 7

Awareness

1 Which of these sentences are correct (C) and incorrect (I)?

1. I'll email you when I get home. ___
2. Sam's going make a pizza tonight. ___
3. Our flight leave at 07.45. ___
4. We'll be lying on the beach this time next week. ___
5. You won't finished by 5 pm. ___
6. He's going to winning this race! ___
7. Donna will meeting you tomorrow. ___
8. I'm not going to help you with this. ___
9. Don't do anything until I'll get there. ___
10. We'll have lived here for eight years next month. ___

How many did you get right? ☐

Grammar

Future Simple

Affirmative	Negative	Questions
I/he/she/it/we/you/they **will** work	I/he/she/it/we/you/they **will not (won't)** work	**Will** I/he/she/it/we/you/they work?
Short Answers		
Yes, I/he/she/it/we/you/they **will**.	**No**, I/he/she/it/we/you/they **won't**.	

We use the Future Simple
- for decisions made at the time of speaking.
*I'**ll answer** the phone.*
- for predictions without having evidence.
*Everyone **will live** to be over 100 years old in the future.*
- promises.
*I promise I'**ll buy** you a new laptop next week.*
- threats.
*Behave yourself or I'**ll tell** the teacher.*
- to talk about future facts.
*The games **will begin** on 9 June.*
- after verbs like *think, believe, be sure, expect,* etc and words like *probably, maybe,* etc.
*I think they'**ll deliver** the keyboards tomorrow.*
- to offer to do something for someone.
*I'**ll pick** you up at the station if you like.*
- to ask someone to do something.
***Will** you **lock** the door when you leave, please?*

> **Note**
>
> We use *shall* with *I* and *we* in questions or when we want to make a suggestion or an offer.
>
> *What website **shall we** visit?*
> ***Shall we** go to the technology fair?*
> ***Shall I** show you how to do a search?*

Be Going To

Affirmative	Negative	Questions
I **am ('m) going to** work he/she/it **is ('s) going to** work we/you/they **are ('re) going to** work	I **am ('m) not going to** work he/she/it **is not (isn't) going to** work we/you/they **are not (aren't) going to** work	**Am** I **going to** work? **Is** he/she/it **going to** work? **Are** we/you/they **going to** work?
Short Answers		
Yes, I **am**. **Yes**, we/you/they **are**. **Yes**, he/she/it **is**.	**No**, I'm **not**. **No**, we/you/they **aren't**. **No**, he/she/it **isn't**.	

We use *be going to* for
- future plans.
*I'**m going to buy** a printer at the weekend.*
- predictions for the near future based on present situations or evidence.
*I'm exhausted. I'**m going to go** home.*

> **Note**
> Some common time expressions that are often used with the Future Simple and *be going to* are *this week/month/summer, tonight, this evening, tomorrow, tomorrow morning/afternoon/night, next week/month/year, at the weekend, in January, in a few minutes/hours/days, on Thursday, on Wednesday morning*, etc.
> *It's okay, I'll check the database **tomorrow morning**.*

Future Continuous

Affirmative	Negative	Questions
I/he/she/it/we/you/they **will be** work**ing**	I/he/she/it/we/you/they **will not (won't) be** work**ing**	**Will** I/he/she/it/we/you/they **be** work**ing**?
Short Answers		
Yes, I/he/she/it/we/you/they **will**.	**No**, I/he/she/it/we/you/they **won't**.	

Spelling: dance → dan**cing**, travel → travel**ling**, tidy → ti**dying**

We use the Future Continuous for
• actions that will be in progress at a specific time in the future.
*We**'ll be learning** about cloning this afternoon.*
• plans and arrangements for the future.
*Tina **will be joining** us for dinner.*

> **Note**
> Some common time expressions that are often used with the Future Continuous are *this time next week/month/summer, this time tomorrow morning/afternoon/night*, etc.
> ***This time next month**, we'll be sitting in our new classroom.*

Future Perfect Simple

Affirmative	Negative	Questions
I/he/she/it/we/you/they **will have** work**ed**	I/he/she/it/we/you/they **will not (won't) have** work**ed**	**Will** I/he/she/it/we/you/they **have** work**ed**?
Short Answers		
Yes, I/he/she/it/we/you/they **will**.	**No**, I/he/she/it/we/you/they **won't**.	

Spelling: walk → walk**ed**, dance → danc**ed**, travel → travel**led**, tidy → ti**died**, play → play**ed**

We use the Future Perfect Simple to talk about
• something that will be finished by or before a specific time in the future.
*I**'ll have finished** designing this website **by** Wednesday.*
• the length of time that an action will have lasted for at a point of time in the future.
*They**'ll have been married** for 40 years **at** the end of this month.*

> **Note**
> Some verbs are irregular and do not follow these spelling rules. See a list of irregular verbs and their past participles on pages 142-143.

> **Note**
> Some common time expressions that are often used with the Future Perfect Simple are *by the end of this week/month/year, by this time tomorrow, by tomorrow morning / ten o'clock / 2012*, etc.
> ***By the end of the week**, I'll have finished all my exams.*

> **Note**
> Other tenses that describe the future are the Present Simple for timetabled events, and the Present Continuous for plans and arrangements.
> *The train to Birmingham **leaves** at 9.45.*
> *John **is coming** to stay this weekend.*

Unit 7 39

Unit 7

Grammar Exercises

2 Circle the correct words.

1 Robots **will be / are being** rulers of the whole world.
2 **Will / Shall** I help you with that?
3 Don't phone me after lunch because I **will sleep / will be sleeping**.
4 By this time tomorrow, they **are finishing / will have finished** decorating.
5 In 100 years time, humans **will be living / are going to live** on Mars.
6 Watch out! That fence **will fall / is going to fall**.
7 **Will / Shall** you do the washing-up, please?
8 It's late. I **will be / am** leaving.
9 I'm sure they **'ll / 're going to** understand.

3 Complete the sentences with the correct form of the Future Simple or Future Continuous of the verbs in brackets.

1 I _____ (lend) you my laptop, if you like.
2 We _____ (sit) on a plane this time tomorrow.
3 I expect Greg _____ (be) home by now.
4 _____ (you / turn on) the light, please?
5 Come and visit when you want. I _____ (not do) anything important.
6 Everyone in the world _____ (have) a computer by 2020.
7 Don't call him between 7.30 and 8.00 because he _____ (watch) his favourite show.
8 _____ (you / eat) dinner in the restaurant this evening, madam?

4 Complete the dialogue with the correct form of the Future Simple of the verbs in brackets or **be going to**.

Sam: Hi Julie. Do you want to come to the town centre with me?
Julie: Have you seen the weather forecast? It **(1)** _____ (rain).
Sam: That's OK – I **(2)** _____ (bring) an umbrella. Come on! I think Dan and Sally **(3)** _____ (be) there.
Julie: I don't care. I **(4)** _____ (stay) in today.
Sam: Oh, come on, Julie. I **(5)** _____ (pick) you up on my scooter.
Julie: No. I **(6)** _____ (sit) on the sofa with my laptop and play games all afternoon.
Sam: What game **(7)** _____ (you / play)?
Julie: I think I **(8)** _____ (try) the new Spiderman game my dad gave me.
Sam: Oh, that's cool.
Julie: Do you want to come round?
Sam: I **(9)** _____ (get) my coat!

5 Complete the sentences with the correct form of the Future Perfect Simple or Future Continuous of the verbs in brackets.

1 By December, I _____ (have) this same computer for six years.
2 In the year 2050, all human beings _____ (live) under water.
3 When I'm sixty, I still _____ (not learn) everything about robotics.
4 This time next year, I _____ (study) physics at university.
5 Maybe touch-screen computers _____ (replace) books in the classroom by 2020.
6 At the end of this term, Mrs Jones _____ (work) through the whole course book with us.
7 Please don't phone me tonight – I _____ (do) my homework until bedtime.
8 We aren't late. The match _____ (not start) yet.

6 Choose the correct answers.

1 From next year, we ___ in a house nearer my school.
   a will live
   b will be living
   c will have lived
2 ___ cooking by seven o'clock?
   a Shall you finish
   b Will you be finishing
   c Will you have finished
3 ___ the new internet café in the shopping centre?
   a Shall we try
   b Will we have tried
   c Will we try
4 Don't hit the printer! You ___ it.
   a will be damaging
   b are going to damage
   c will have damaged
5 Do you think Mrs Scott ___ to the head teacher yet?
   a will speak
   b will be speaking
   c will have spoken
6 How long ___ each other by the end of this year?
   a will we know
   b will we be knowing
   c will we have known
7 Be quiet when you get home tonight. We ___.
   a are going to sleep
   b will have slept
   c will be sleeping
8 Relax. The weather ___ fine tomorrow.
   a is going to be
   b will be being
   c will have been

7 Find the mistakes and correct the sentences.

1 I'll giving a talk on the Internet next weekend.

2 By the end of the year, I'll be completing my course.

3 Tom won't be finished the project yet.

4 Shall you help me, please?

5 I'm not going cook this evening.

6 Simon won't have come with us tomorrow.

7 This time next week, I'll shop.

8 Shall I be showing you how to back up your work?

Vocabulary

Word formation

8 Match the words with their meanings.

1 explode
2 excel
3 industry
4 inspire
5 imagine
6 power
7 react
8 revolution

a to do very well at something
b to make someone want to do something
c to create an idea or picture in your mind
d to burst with force
e to do something because something else has been done
f the production of things in factories
g strength
h a very big and important change in society or field of knowledge

Unit 7 41

Unit 7

9 Use the word in capitals to form a word that fits in the gap.

1. Giving students free access to the Internet really _____ them. **POWER**
2. Use your _____ to write a short fictional story. **IMAGINE**
3. This new device will _____ the way people use their mobile phones. **REVOLUTION**
4. The teacher gave an _____ talk to the new students. **INSPIRE**
5. The police closed the roads in the centre of town after the _____. **EXPLODE**
6. That was an _____ film! **EXCEL**
7. Not many people live in the _____ part of the city. **INDUSTRY**
8. What was Ben's _____ when you told him the news? **REACT**

Exam Practice

10 Complete the second sentence so that it has a similar meaning to the first sentence, using the word given. Do not change the word given. You must use between two and five words.

1. I've decided not to do this homework until tomorrow morning.
   going
   I _____ this homework until tomorrow morning.

2. You can phone me before 11 pm because I'll be awake.
   sleeping
   I _____ before 11 pm, so you can phone me.

3. Sam will be there by now, I expect.
   arrived
   I expect Sam _____ by now.

4. What time is the match tomorrow?
   start
   What time _____ tomorrow?

5. My room will be redecorated by Sunday.
   have
   We _____ my room by Sunday.

6. I expect Maria will pass all her exams.
   sure
   I _____ fail any of her exams.

7. Computer science is what he intends to study at university.
   going
   He _____ computer science at university.

8. Five o'clock is when we leave.
   are
   We _____ five o'clock.

11 Complete the sentences with the word that best fits each gap.

1. The phone's ringing. I'll _____ it.
2. What are you going _____ buy Tim for his birthday.
3. I don't think we _____ have finished eating by that time.
4. _____ they going to the internet café?
5. The next flight to Madrid departs _____ 5.15.
6. In five years time, the computer you are using will _____ become useless.
7. Every student will be using this technology in the classroom _____ this time next year.
8. Will _____ be a scanner in my new office?

Writing

12 Write a paragraph in your notebook. Imagine what you will be doing in 15 years time. Say how your life will have changed. How do you think the world will be different?

Unit 8

Awareness

1 Which of these sentences are correct (C) and incorrect (I)?

1. When I finished this game, I'll go home. ___
2. The food will be gone before we get there. ___
3. You can go to the park when you'll do the dishes. ___
4. I'll help you after this show will be over. ___
5. Once everyone is ready, we'll start the game. ___
6. We're not allowed to go out until we've tidied our rooms. ___
7. He's getting a new computer when he'll save enough money. ___
8. After you've done this exercise, you'll feel better. ___
9. She'll have left by the time you got home. ___
10. I let you know as soon as your email arrives. ___

How many did you get right? ☐

Grammar
Temporals

When we use temporals such as *when, before, after, until, once, by the time*, etc to talk about the future, we use them with a present tense. We do not use them with a future tense.
***After** I **have logged off**, I'll go to bed.*
*The shops will be closed **by the time** we **get** into town.*

We use the Present Perfect Simple to emphasise that the first action is finished before the other one starts.
*You can watch TV **when** you**'ve finished** your dinner.* (You'll finish your dinner first and then you'll watch TV.)
***Once** your dad **gets** home, I'll start cooking.* (Dad will get home first and then I'll start.)

Grammar Exercises

2 Circle the correct words.

1. I'm not going out **until / by the time** I've had breakfast.
2. We'll go to the new museum **when / until** it opens.
3. **By the time / The moment** we have the answer, we'll call you.
4. They'll be sleeping **by the time / as soon as** you get here.
5. You'll have to change your shoes **until / before** you go out.
6. **Once / Before** you've finished your exams, we'll celebrate.
7. Don't forget to send me the document **by the time / as soon as** you've finished.
8. He'll want to lie down **after / until** his race is over.

Unit 8

3 Complete the sentences with the correct form of the Present Simple or Future Simple of these verbs.

arrive   buy   give   leave   open   see   send   speak

1 Let's wait here until the café _____.
2 I _____ you my phone number before I go.
3 What are you going to do when you _____ school?
4 We _____ him an email as soon as we know his exam results.
5 You'd better tidy up before your mother _____ home.
6 Once we've moved to our new house, we _____ some new furniture.
7 The doctor _____ you as soon as he's ready.
8 Give Tonya this note when you _____ to her, please.

4 Complete the sentences with the correct form of the Present Simple or Future Simple of the verbs in brackets.

1 We like to play tennis when the weather _____ (be) nice.
2 Let's go home before it _____ (start) raining.
3 I _____ (tell) you all about my day when I get back.
4 Judy _____ (write) her report once she has gathered all the information.
5 When I get my new mobile, I _____ (be) able to send photos to my friends.
6 We _____ (wait) until you have wi-fi before we _____ (come) and visit you.
7 _____ (you / have) a shower before you _____ (go) out tonight?
8 I _____ (ask) him the next time I _____ (see) him.

5 Choose the correct answers.

1 Don't go out until the rain __.
   a stopped
   b will stop
   c stops
2 Will you visit us __ you are in the country?
   a when
   b before
   c until
3 I __ you my new camera when I see you.
   a show
   b 'll show
   c 've shown
4 Do you want a drink before you __ to bed?
   a go
   b 'll go
   c 've gone
5 You're not leaving __ you answer my question.
   a when
   b until
   c once
6 I'll have a bath __ I get home.
   a the moment
   b until
   c by the time
7 She __ sad when she finally leaves school.
   a 's
   b 'll be
   c 's been
8 I __ this by the end of next week.
   a 'll finished
   b 'll have finished
   c finished

6 Complete the sentences with the word that best fits each gap.

1 Will you _____ completed this by five o'clock?
2 They should be ready _____ the time we get there.
3 I think I'll fall asleep _____ moment my head touches the pillow.
4 She _____ have finished breakfast before she goes for her run.
5 Tell him to wait there _____ I've spoken to his teacher.
6 As _____ as the sun comes out, we'll go to the park.

44

7 Complete the sentences.

1. You'll pass all your exams. We'll have a party then.
   We'll have a party when you pass all your exams.
2. I'll get a new mobile phone. I'll give you my number.
   I _____ as soon as _____.
3. My dad must give me permission first. I won't go out until then.
   _____ until _____.
4. You'll arrive this evening. But the children will already be in bed.
   By the time _____.
5. The technician must fix the computers. Then we'll start work again.
   We _____ once _____.
6. A thunder storm is going to start. Let's go back to the car before it does.
   _____ before _____.
7. I'll buy some food. Then I'll come home and cook.
   _____ when _____.
8. This film will end. Then we will go for a drive.
   _____ after _____.

Vocabulary

Phrasal verbs

8 Match the phrasal verbs with their meanings.

1. back up
2. back out
3. blast off
4. come up with
5. hook up
6. log in
7. set off
8. set up

a. to begin a journey
b. to connect to a power supply
c. (of a rocket) to leave the earth and head for space
d. to save a copy of your work
e. to prepare or organise
f. to think of and create something new
g. to decide not to do something you had arranged to do
h. to gain access to a computer

9 Complete the sentences with the correct form of the phrasal verbs from 8.

1. The rocket is due to _____ into the atmosphere at 5.00.
2. Can you _____ a meeting for next Tuesday afternoon?
3. If we _____ at 8 am, we will get to the station before nine.
4. The printer didn't work because it wasn't _____ to the computer.
5. We didn't know what to do until Sammy _____ a brilliant idea.
6. Always _____ your work! You'll lose it if you don't.
7. I'm sorry, I'm going to have to _____ of this project – I've got too much work to do.
8. The network is down, so I can't _____ to my account at the moment.

Unit 8

Unit 8

Exam Practice

10 Complete the second sentence so that it has a similar meaning to the first sentence, using the word given. Do not change the word given. You must use between two and five words.

1. I'll only help you if you apologise to Rachel.
   until
   I won't _____ you apologise to Rachel.

2. She's saving her money to buy a laptop.
   when
   She'll _____ has saved enough money.

3. They're not there yet because they left late.
   set
   They _____, so they're not there yet.

4. When you get to school, go and see the head teacher immediately.
   soon
   Go and see the head teacher _____ to school.

5. We're going to stay here until we can find a solution.
   come
   We're not leaving until _____ a solution.

6. As soon as I left the house it started to rain.
   moment
   It started to rain _____ the house.

7. I'll log off after I've backed up my work.
   before
   I'll _____ I log off.

8. When we get there, the party will be over.
   time
   The party will be over _____ get there.

11 Use the word in capitals to form a word that fits in the gap.

1. What a _____ teacher Mrs Simpson is! — **MARVEL**
2. There have been some interesting _____ in the world of computer science. — **DEVELOP**
3. Her father is a _____ for the town council. — **RESEARCH**
4. We want to _____ young people to train for a career in computer programming. — **COURAGE**
5. The world's first computer is now just a _____ in a museum. — **CURIOUS**
6. Are you _____ about the future? — **OPTIMIST**
7. Astronauts become _____ when they leave the Earth's gravitational field. — **WEIGHT**
8. That's the most _____ story I've ever heard. I don't believe it. — **CREDIBLE**

Writing

12 In your notebook, write
- two things you will do when you get home from school tomorrow.
- two things you will do before you are 20.
- two things you will have done by the time you are 30.
- two things you want to do after you are 50.

Review 2

Grammar

1 Complete the email with the correct form of the Present Perfect Simple or Present Perfect Continuous of the verbs in brackets.

> **Inbox**
>
> Hi Martin,
>
> Well, we **(1)** _____ (be) here in Scotland for three days now. It's the first holiday we **(2)** _____ (have) since 2010! Unfortunately, it **(3)** _____ (rain) for the past two days, and we **(4)** _____ (not leave) the hotel yet.
>
> Dad **(5)** _____ (complain) non-stop since we arrived. He just wants to go out and play golf. I don't think he'll be good at it because he **(6)** _____ (not play) for years. I **(7)** _____ (read) the latest book by my favourite author. I **(8)** _____ (not finish) it yet, but it's great.
>
> Maria **(9)** _____ (just / come) into the room. Her hair is wet because she **(10)** _____ (swim). At least there's an indoor swimming pool here – so that keeps her happy. I don't know what I'm going to do when I **(11)** _____ (read) my book. I hope the weather changes soon!
>
> Best wishes,
>
> Tony

2 Complete the sentences with these words. Use **a/an** where necessary.

> experience   medicine   food   goal   illness   sugar   diet   advice

1 When I'm ill, I usually take _____.
2 Terry scored _____ the last time he played football.
3 She's never suffered from _____ in her life.
4 When I have a problem, I always ask my grandmother for _____.
5 I'm hungry. I need _____.
6 You're looking a bit overweight – maybe you should go on _____.
7 Do you like _____ in your coffee?
8 Spending a week in hospital was _____ I don't want to repeat.

3 Choose the correct answers.

1 ___ work by nine o'clock?
  a Will you be starting
  b Will you have started
  c Shall you start

2 ___ to the cinema tonight?
  a Shall we go
  b Will we have gone
  c Do we go

3 Don't worry. Everything ___ alright.
  a is going to be
  b will have been
  c will be being

4 Do you think the match ___ yet?
  a will finish
  b will be finishing
  c will have finished

5 Don't play football in the house! You ___ something.
  a 'll be breaking
  b 're going to break
  c 'll have broken

6 How long ___ here by the end of this year?
  a will you work
  b will you be working
  c will you have worked

7 This time next week, we ___.
  a 're going to sunbathe
  b 'll be sunbathing
  c 'll have sunbathed

8 Computers ___ more intelligent than humans soon.
  a will be
  b will have been
  c are being

Review 2

4 Complete the sentences with the correct form of the Present Simple or Future Simple of the verbs in brackets.

1 I _____ (check) the computer for viruses before you _____ (start) using it, just to be safe.
2 The children _____ (have to) have a shower as soon as they _____ (get) back from their camping trip.
3 The moment it _____ (start) to rain, the tennis match _____ (be) stopped.
4 We _____ (wait) until the weather _____ (improve), then we _____ (leave).
5 When I _____ (get) my new bike, I _____ (ride) to school every day.
6 Once I _____ (know) what time the train is, I _____ (tell) you if I can pick you up.
7 Jenny _____ (buy) a new house when her prize money _____ (arrive).
8 They _____ (call) us the moment they _____ (hear) any news about the accident.

5 Find the mistakes and correct the sentences.

1 Would you like a help with your homework?

2 He's been run in the park.

3 I've taken just some cough medicine.

4 What time are you going deliver the pizza?

5 She's been doing gymnastics since three years.

6 I'll phone you after I'll make the dinner.

7 They yet won't have finished.

8 Let me give you an advice.

6 Circle the correct words.

1 I **have slept / slept** well last night.
2 Greg has been playing games **all morning / yesterday morning**.
3 Would you like **a / some** milk?
4 **Shall / Will** I walk with you to the bus stop?
5 You can go out **when / until** you have done the dishes.
6 We'll **have known / be knowing** each other for two years next week.
7 Don't call her now. She **sleeps / will be sleeping**.
8 I've made **some / any** cakes for your party.

Exam Practice

7 For questions 1–10, read the text below. Use the word given in capitals at the end of each line to form a word that fits in the gap in the same line. There is an example at the beginning (0).

The urban poor

As well as being places of great (0) ___economic___ wealth, big cities are places   ECONOMY
where poverty exists on a large scale. It is a problem for which there has not yet been found
a (1) _____. There are, of course, poor people in country areas, but that   SOLVE
is where the (2) _____ ends.   SIMILAR
The poor in urban areas are considered (3) _____ and are more likely to   FAIL
suffer from (4) _____ than the poor in rural areas. The situation of the rural   ILL
poor is regarded as (5) _____ because there are very few opportunities for   AVOID
them to improve their lives. This is not (6) _____ believed to be the case   GENERAL
with the urban poor, who are often blamed for the sorry state of their own lives. Their spirits
weakened, the urban poor begin to accept their (7) _____ conditions as   LIFE
their fate. Eventually, many may become susceptible to (8) _____.   DEPRESS
Some, unable to face the (9) _____ prospect of a life without hope,   TERROR
turn to drugs or alcohol. At this point, anyone trying to help them out of their situation will
face great (10) _____ in getting through to them.   DIFFICULT

8 For questions 11–22, read the text below and think of the word which best fits each gap. Use only one word in each gap. There is an example at the beginning (0).

Kuala Lumpur: A city of contrasts

Kuala Lumpur is the (0) __ of Malaysia and probably the city in Asia which has changed most in the (11) __ fifteen years. It now (12) __ a relaxed, colonial atmosphere with space age technology, making it (13) __ among developing Asian cities.

Fifteen years ago Kuala Lumpur was just a (14) __ of colonial buildings and gardens. Most of the business in the (15) __ was carried out in Hong Kong, China or Singapore. At that time Kuala Lumpur was in (16) __ of being left behind the other big far eastern cities.

Nowadays Kuala Lumpur is world class – something which the whole (17) __ is proud of. But although remarkable progress has been (18) __, the Malaysians still have a need to be recognised by the whole world. They have made plans to achieve this, and are determined to (19) __ them through. That is why they are always seeking to improve their standard of living by (20) __ only the very best.

However, success has brought with it certain problems. Traffic sometimes creates a deadly smog which the locals refuse to (21) __ on, and the Western media has a habit of criticising the city. (22) __ these kinds of problems, the Malaysians remain determined to reach the top.

0	A	leading	B	primary	C	first	**D**	**capital**
11	A	latest	B	later	C	last	D	recent
12	A	shares	B	connects	C	sticks	D	combines
13	A	single	B	unique	C	separate	D	solitary
14	A	collection	B	bundle	C	bunch	D	pack
15	A	region	B	territory	C	place	D	location
16	A	risk	B	emergency	C	danger	D	jeopardy
17	A	race	B	tribe	C	people	D	nation
18	A	done	B	carried	C	taken	D	made
19	A	take	B	see	C	put	D	run
20	A	asking	B	persisting	C	insisting	D	demanding
21	A	mention	B	comment	C	refer	D	discuss
22	A	Despite	B	Although	C	However	D	But

Review 2

Grammar

9 For questions 1–10, choose the word or phrase that best completes the sentence or conversation.

1 Only ___ people came to my party.
 A many
 B a little
 C a lot of
 D a few

2 'Oh, there you are!'
 'Have you ___ for me?'
 A been looking
 B look
 C looking
 D looked

3 'Can you give me some money?'
 'Sorry, I don't have ___.'
 A some
 B none
 C any
 D few

4 He will win if he ___ fast enough.
 A 'll run
 B runs
 C ran
 D running

5 I'm not speaking to him ___ he apologises.
 A when
 B once
 C because
 D until

6 'How's your headache?'
 'I ___ an aspirin, so I'll feel better soon.'
 A just have taken
 B 've taken just
 C just taken
 D 've just taken

7 Would you like a ___ of cheese?
 A jar
 B piece
 C loaf
 D can

8 'Look at Laura. She looks ill.'
 'Oh dear. She ___ sick.'
 A 'll be
 B 'll have been
 C 'll be being
 D 's going to be

9 James ___ to lunch tomorrow, isn't he?
 A comes
 B is coming
 C will come
 D has come

10 Do you think the children ___ lunch yet?
 A will have eaten
 B are going to eat
 C ate
 D eat

Vocabulary

10 For questions 11–20, choose the word or phrase that best completes the sentence or conversation.

11 Have you been vaccinated ___ the flu?
 A against
 B on
 C over
 D to

12 I need a holiday to recharge my ___.
 A brains
 B legs
 C daisy
 D batteries

13 You'll lose your work if you don't back it ___.
 A off
 B on
 C out
 D up

14 Do you want to ___ to our collection?
 A focus
 B contribute
 C work
 D intend

15 I feel really ___ the weather today.
 A under
 B over
 C off
 D by

16 Try this medicine. It'll do you the ___ of good.
 A universe
 B earth
 C world
 D planet

17 Daniel has ___ up with a brilliant plan!
 A gone
 B come
 C run
 D made

18 He ___ up a computer repair company eight years ago.
 A worked
 B had
 C lifted
 D set

19 'I'm worried about Maria.'
 'Don't worry. She'll be back on her ___ in no time!'
 A feet
 B arms
 C bed
 D legs

20 The rocket is due to blast ___ at 11.30.
 A up
 B out
 C off
 D over

50

Unit 9

Awareness

1 Which of these sentences are correct (C) and incorrect (I)?

1. You needn't read this if you don't want to. ___
2. He ought to eating more fruit. ___
3. People can be happy and poor. ___
4. We must to try our best at all times. ___
5. She may be succeed in the world of finance. ___
6. He can't be 18! ___
7. I think she might be right. ___
8. Could you speaking a little bit louder, please? ___
9. No, you mayn't eat the last biscuit. ___
10. We were able to get tickets at the last minute. ___

How many did you get right? ☐

Grammar

Can & Could

We use *can* + bare infinitive
• to talk about general ability in the present and the future.
Susan **can ride** a bike.
• for requests.
Can you **give** me some help?
• for permission.
Yes, you **can go out** tonight.

We use *can't* + bare infinitive to show that we are sure that something isn't true.
Mrs Smith **can't be** on holiday. I've just seen her.

We use *could* + bare infinitive
• to talk about general ability in the past. (past form of *can*)
George **could play** the piano when he was three.
• to talk about possibility.
He **could lose** his job.
• for polite requests.
Could you **close** the door please?
• to make suggestions.
You **could take** extra lessons in the evening.

May & Might

We use *may* + bare infinitive
• to talk about possibility in the future.
She **may decide** not to go to university.
• for polite requests. (with *I* and *we*)
May I **sit** here?
• for polite permission.
Yes, you **may bring** your friend with you.

We use *might* + bare infinitive
• to talk about possibility in the future.
I **might get** a job abroad.
• as the past tense of *may*.
She said she **might buy** a new car.

Unit 9

Must

We use *must* + bare infinitive to
- say that something is necessary.
*I **must go** to the bank before it closes.*
- talk about obligations.
*You **must leave** the building by five o'clock.*
- show that we are sure that something is true.
*She **must be** very rich – look at her car!*
- recommend something.
*You **must see** this film.*

We use *mustn't* + bare infinitive to talk about something that is not allowed.
*You **mustn't use** your mobile phone in the library.*

Should

We use *should* + bare infinitive to
- give advice.
*You **should do** the best you can.*
- ask for advice.
***Should** I **apply** for this job?*

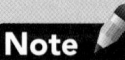

Note

Ought to can also be used to give advice, but it is not usually used in the question form.
*You **ought to study** a bit harder.*

Would

We use *would* + bare infinitive for
- actions that we did regularly in the past, but that we don't do now.
*We **would** often **have** lunch in the park.*
- polite requests.
***Would** you **do** me a favour, please?*

Needn't

We use *needn't* + bare infinitive to say that something is not necessary.
*You **needn't finish** this work tonight. Tomorrow will be fine.*

Note

We can also use *need* as an ordinary verb. It has affirmative, negative and question forms and it is usually used in the Present Simple and the Past Simple. It is followed by a full infinitive.
*She **needs to try** harder.*
*He doesn't **need to ask** permission to do anything.*
***Do** we **need to get** anything from the market?*

Be Able To

We use *be able to* to talk about
- general ability.
*We **are able to move** from place to place quite easily.*
- a specific ability in the past. (*Could* cannot be used here.)
*I **was able to complete** the questionnaire.*

Have To

We use *have to* to
- say that something is necessary.
*We **have to hand in** our projects at the end of the week.*
*Does she **have to prepare** the food for the party?*
- talk about obligation.
*Do you **have to do** any work around the house?*

Mustn't & Don't Have To

There is an important difference between *mustn't* and *don't have to*. We use *mustn't* to say that something is not allowed, whereas we use *don't have to* to show that there is no obligation or necessity.
*You **mustn't take** photos in the museum.*
*You **don't have to come** with us tonight. You can stay at home if you want.*

Grammar Exercises

2 Circle the correct answers.

1 I'm glad I **can / was able to** speak to you before you left.
2 **Can I / Am I able to** help you with anything, madam?
3 She'd love to **can / be able to** make a lot of money.
4 **Can / Could** you hear the cats fighting outside last night?
5 Fortunately, my parents **can / were able to** buy their own house shortly before I was born.
6 Our hotel was beautiful, and we **can / could** see the whole city from our window.
7 No, sorry. You **can't / aren't able to** borrow my laptop – I need it.
8 **Can you / Are you able to** do this exercise easily?

3 Complete the sentences with must, mustn't or don't / doesn't have to.

1 Steve _____ work because he is very rich.
2 You _____ be late, or you will be in trouble.
3 All students _____ complete their projects by 6 April.
4 My grandparents _____ travel far to visit us – they only live around the corner.
5 You _____ bring animals into the hospital. It's not allowed.
6 The law in the UK says that motorcyclists _____ always wear a helmet when riding.
7 Children _____ play with fire – it's dangerous!
8 You _____ get up early tomorrow. You can stay in bed all day if you feel like it!

4 Complete the sentences with can't be or must be.

1 Dan _____ at home. I've called and there's no answer.
2 That café _____ very good. There's never anybody in it!
3 Susan is going to New York tomorrow. She _____ looking forward to it.
4 I hear Dave failed all his exams. He _____ very happy about that.
5 Nobody has bought that house yet. It _____ too expensive.
6 It _____ a great show, because it's nearly impossible to get tickets for it.
7 That _____ Jack at the door – he's still in Germany.
8 Sara _____ ill, because she isn't at school and she hates missing lessons.

5 Choose the correct answers.

1 ___ I ask you a personal question?
  a Must
  b May
  c Needn't

2 Trevor ___ write his name until he was six. That's quite late.
  a couldn't
  b can't
  c mustn't

3 It ___ be easy to work 12 hours a day, seven days a week.
  a shouldn't
  b can't
  c mustn't

4 You ___ succeed if you work hard enough.
  a can't
  b must
  c may

5 She ___ be very clever to go to university at the age of 16.
  a must
  b can
  c should

6 People ___ leave litter in the park – it's not fair on others.
  a couldn't
  b might not
  c shouldn't

7 Burglars ___ to get in through a window last night.
  a can
  b could
  c were able

8 You ___ worry about your future. I'm sure you'll be successful.
  a can't
  b needn't
  c couldn't

Unit 9 53

Unit 9

6 Complete the dialogues with the correct form of these modal verbs.

A can   can't   don't have to   might   mustn't   should

Judy: I'm worried about Tim. It's 10 pm and he isn't home yet. What **(1)** _____ I do?
Thomas: You **(2)** _____ worry, I'm sure he's fine. He **(3)** _____ be at Maria's house – did you phone her?
Judy: He **(4)** _____ be at Maria's house. She's in France with her family.
Thomas: Oh.
Judy: **(5)** _____ I borrow your phone? I want to call his friend, Mark.
Thomas: It's okay. You **(6)** _____ borrow my phone. Here he comes now!

B can't   can   couldn't   must   might

Joel: Look, Mum. I **(1)** _____ do tricks on my skateboard.
Sarah: Be careful, Joel – you **(2)** _____ hurt yourself.
Simon: He **(3)** _____ be a talented boy. I **(4)** _____ do tricks like that when I was his age. They're really difficult!
Sarah: I don't know where he gets his talent from. It **(5)** _____ be me – I'm no good at things like that.

7 Complete the sentences with the word that best fits each gap.

1 I'll _____ to buy a new swimming costume before we go on holiday.
2 You _____ not speak during the test, or you'll be asked to leave.
3 I always go to my aunt for advice. She tells me what I _____ do.
4 We don't have _____ go to school today.
5 When Paula was a little girl, she _____ able to run for miles without getting tired.
6 Dad _____ to work late last night, so he didn't get home until midnight.
7 My careers advisor thinks I _____ to consider joining the army.
8 She _____ not want us to come and visit her, so call her first.

Vocabulary

Prepositions

8 Complete the phrases with these prepositions. You will need to use some prepositions more than once.

at   from   of   to

1 according _____
2 to be banned _____
3 to be good _____
4 to dream _____
5 to spread _____
6 to be different _____
7 to be surprised _____
8 to make a success _____

9 Complete the sentences with the correct form of the phrases from 8.

1 _____ researchers, rich people are not much happier than poor people.
2 If you work hard enough, you'll _____ anything you do.
3 I was very _____ the price of the jacket. I didn't expect it to be so expensive.
4 When I was a child, I used to _____ being an astronaut.
5 Danny _____ going out at playtime for a week because of his behaviour.
6 The reason I don't like basketball is because I'm not very _____ it.
7 The virus quickly _____ every computer on the network.
8 I'm quite similar to my brother, but I'm completely _____ my sister.

Exam Practice

10 Complete the second sentence so that it has a similar meaning to the first sentence, using the word given. Do not change the word given. You must use between two and five words.

1 It isn't necessary for you to eat all your dinner.
  have
  You _____ all your dinner.

2 Playing football is prohibited here.
  must
  You _____ here.

3 I'm sure George isn't at school today.
  be
  George _____ today.

4 It is possible that it'll rain tomorrow.
  might
  It _____ tomorrow.

5 It wasn't necessary for him to pay for his lunch.
  have
  He _____ for his lunch.

6 I advise you to go and see a doctor.
  ought
  You _____ a doctor.

7 I hope you have a successful time at university.
  make
  I hope _____ your time at university.

8 These two computer games are not at all similar.
  from
  This computer game is very _____ that one.

11 Use the word in capitals to form a word that fits in the gap.

1 I was surprised by the teacher's _____ request. USUAL
2 She caught a nasty disease while abroad, but fortunately it was easily _____. TREAT
3 He _____ completed the course. SUCCEED
4 Be warned that staring at the sun can cause _____. BLIND
5 My father is a very _____ person in newspaper journalism. INFLUENCE
6 Are you _____ about the future? OPTIMIST
7 Although she was a successful businesswoman, everyone was impressed by her _____. MODEST
8 His only ambition is to be _____ before he gets old. WEALTH

Writing

12 What are the rules? In your notebook, write some rules for your perfect school. Write
- three things that students have to do.
- three things that students don't have to do.
- three things that students mustn't do.

Unit 10

Awareness

1 Which of these sentences are correct (C) and incorrect (I)?

1. Simon should have tried harder. ___
2. My company could have been successful. ___
3. I would helped you if I could. ___
4. Should I invited Tim to the party? ___
5. They might left earlier. ___
6. That must have been a difficult decision to make. ___
7. You can't have finish already! ___
8. Could Megan have been upset about her results? ___
9. I needn't have sold my bike. ___
10. You could have succeed if you had tried harder. ___

How many did you get right? ☐

Grammar

May/Might Have

We use *may/might have* + past participle to show that we are not sure about something in the past.
Steve **may have heard** the news already.

Should Have

We use *should have* + past participle
• to show that something we were expecting did not happen.
The children **should have arrived** home by now.
• to criticise our own or someone else's behaviour.
You **shouldn't have tried** to climb on the roof!

Could Have

We use *could have* + past participle to
• show that we are not sure about something in the past.
I **could have** left my keys on the table in the hall.
• say that something was possible in the past, but that it didn't happen.
He **could have** been a successful businessman, but he became a teacher instead.

Can't/Couldn't Have

We use *can't/couldn't have* + past participle to show that we are sure that something is not true about the past.
Dan **can't have won** the gold medal – he is not fast enough.

Must Have

We use *must have* + past participle to show that we are sure that something is true about the past.
You **must have been** surprised when the parcel arrived.

Would Have

We use *would have* + past participle to say that we were willing to do something, but that we didn't do it.
I **would have lent** him the money if I had it.

Needn't Have

We use *needn't have* + past participle to say it wasn't necessary to do something but you did it anyway.
You **needn't have rushed**. The show has been cancelled.

Grammar Exercises

2 Circle the correct words.
1. I think I might **have / had** forgotten to close the windows.
2. You **could / must** have won that prize if you had bought a ticket.
3. Sam **shouldn't / mustn't** have spoken to me like that.
4. She **can / can't have** finished her work already.
5. Oh dear, I think I **would / might** have made a mistake.
6. We **could / must** have gone with them, but we didn't feel like it.
7. The car is not here – it **can / must** have been stolen.
8. We all did the wrong homework, so the teacher **mustn't / couldn't** have explained it clearly.
9. **Would / Should** you have preferred to have studied a different subject at university?
10. He **can't / mustn't** have forgotten his lunch money again!

3 Use the prompts to write sentences.
1. studied / might / She / at school / German / have
   _____
2. may / received / not / Simon / have / his invitation
   _____
3. a great idea / That / been / not / have / might
   _____
4. late home / We / be / may / tonight
   _____
5. become / have / She / a famous singer / might
   _____
6. may / an accident / There / been / have
   _____
7. not / Jane / ready / been / have / might
   _____
8. gone / to the library / He / already / may / have
   _____

Unit 10

4 Complete the email with these modals and the correct form of the verbs in brackets.

can't   might   must   should   shouldn't   would

> Inbox
>
> Dear Dan
>
> Congratulations on passing all your exams this year. You **(1)** _____ (be) delighted when you found out!
>
> Unfortunately, Gill didn't do as well as you. She **(2)** _____ (study) a bit harder, in my opinion – and she **(3)** _____ (go) out with her friends every night! She's not stupid, and I'm certain she **(4)** _____ (pass) if she'd tried.
>
> She's still upset. It **(5)** _____ (be) easy for her when she heard that you had passed them all. I'm hoping that she **(6)** _____ (learn) her lesson now, and will try harder next year.
>
> Love,
>
> Aunt Sally

5 Complete the sentences with **can't have** or **must have** and the past participle of the verbs in brackets.

1. She _____ (know) the answer to the question, because she left it blank.
2. Sue looks tired – she _____ (go) to bed late last night.
3. They _____ (enjoy) their meal because they didn't eat half of it.
4. You _____ (forget) to invite Tonya, because she says she didn't know about it.
5. Katy said the exam was really easy. She _____ (study) a lot for it.
6. It _____ (be) Mrs Green who you saw in town, because she's been dead for two years.
7. Ben _____ (steal) the money. He's a very honest boy.
8. Somebody _____ (call) a taxi because there's one waiting outside.

6 Complete the sentences using **should have** or **shouldn't have**.

1. You didn't wait for me.
   You should have waited for me.
2. He lied to me.
   He _____.
3. She broke her promise.
   She _____.
4. We didn't say thank you to you.
   We _____.
5. I was late for my piano lesson.
   I _____.
6. My uncle didn't buy my sister a birthday present.
   My uncle _____.
7. The boys ate too much chocolate cake.
   The boys _____.
8. She didn't apologise.
   She _____.

7 Write sentences with needn't have.

1 You brought flowers! That wasn't necessary.
   You needn't have brought flowers.
2 We went shopping for food. We already had plenty.
   We _____.
3 He called to say he was late. I already knew that.
   He _____.
4 I got up early this morning. There was nothing to do.
   I _____.
5 She studied hard, but the exam was easy.
   She _____.
6 They were worried. There was nothing to worry about.
   They _____.
7 I gave her my umbrella. It didn't rain.
   I _____.
8 Charlie took the medicine. He wasn't ill.
   Charlie _____.

Vocabulary

Collocations & Expressions

8 Put the words into the correct column.

a profit   bankrupt   business   chances   into partnership   progress   your best   your place

go	_____	_____
do	_____	_____
make	_____	_____
take	_____	_____

9 Complete the sentences with the correct form of the phrases from 8.

1 If you're willing to _____, that means you are prepared to risk failure.
2 When you _____ with someone, you agree to work together in the same business.
3 When a business or project is moving forwards, it's _____.
4 The main aim of any business must be to _____, or there would be no point.
5 If someone is employed to do the job you used to do, they're _____.
6 When a business fails completely, it _____.
7 If you _____ with someone, you buy something from them or sell something to them.
8 Always _____ – you can't do any better!

Unit 10

Exam Practice

10 Complete the second sentence so that it has a similar meaning to the first sentence, using the word given. Do not change the word given. You must use between two and five words.

1. Perhaps Amy went to the park
   could
   Amy _____ to the park.

2. It's a pity you didn't ask for her autograph.
   should
   You _____ for her autograph.

3. It was wrong of him to shout at the children.
   shouted
   He _____ at the children.

4. Maybe Maryam didn't want to be in the play.
   might
   Maryam _____ to be in the play.

5. We worried unnecessarily about the weather.
   needn't
   We _____ about the weather.

6. My dad joined my uncle to set up a business.
   partnership
   My dad _____ my uncle to set up a business.

7. I had a ticket, but I didn't want to go to the show.
   could
   I _____ to the show, but I didn't want to.

8. Harry looks happy, so I think his team won the championship.
   must
   Harry's team _____, because he looks happy.

11 Complete the sentences with the word that best fits each gap.

1. If we don't make a profit this month, we'll _____ bankrupt.
2. They might _____ forgotten there's no school today.
3. I think my bike might have _____ stolen.
4. We're looking for someone to _____ your place in the basketball team.
5. The kids must have _____ a great time at the fair.
6. Don't worry about winning – just _____ your best.
7. We're _____ good progress with this project now.
8. He _____ have gone to school if he could, but he was too ill.

Writing

12 Imagine you have arranged to meet a friend at your house, but they still haven't arrived. In your notebook, write five sentences using **might have**, **might not have**, **can't have**, **must have**, and **should have**.

He might have forgotten about it.

Unit 11

Awareness

1 Which of these sentences are correct (C) and incorrect (I)?

1. They had just started eaten when the doorbell rang. ___
2. We had forgotten to put petrol in the car. ___
3. Mandy had been waiting since an hour and a half. ___
4. Had the children been fighting? ___
5. The archeologist had been found something amazing. ___
6. I wanted to go because it had been great fun last time. ___
7. She was tired because she had running. ___
8. I was surprised that you hadn't been hearing the story before. ___
9. They hadn't seen the first film, so it was hard to understand the second. ___
10. We had been playing computer games for about nine o'clock that morning. ___

How many did you get right? ☐

Grammar
Past Perfect Simple

Affirmative	Negative	Questions
I/he/she/it/we/you/they **had** (**'d**) lived	I/he/she/it/we/you/they **had not** (**hadn't**) lived	**Had** I/he/she/it/we/you/they liv**ed**?
Short Answers		
Yes, I/he/she/it/we/you/they **had**.	No, I/he/she/it/we/you/they **hadn't**.	

Spelling: walk → walk**ed**, love → lov**ed**, travel → trave**lled**, stu**dy** → stu**died**, play → play**ed**

We use the Past Perfect Simple for an action or situation that finished before another action, situation or time in the past.
They **had read** all of the Harry Potter books **before they watched** the films.
By the time she was five, she **had learned** to skateboard.

Note
Some verbs are irregular and do not follow these spelling rules. See a list of irregular verbs and their past participles on pages 142–143.

Note
Some common time expressions that are often used with the Past Perfect Simple are *before, after, when, already, for, for a long time, for ages, just, never, once, since 2009/July, yet*, etc.

I hadn't picked up a guitar **for weeks** *because of my broken finger.*

Unit 11

Past Perfect Continuous

Affirmative	Negative	Questions
I/he/she/it/we/you/they **had** (**'d**) **been** living	I/he/she/it/we/you/they **had not** (**hadn't**) **been** living	**Had** I/he/she/it/we/you/they **been** living?
Short Answers		
Yes, I/he/she/it/we/you/they **had**.	**No**, I/he/she/it/we/you/they **hadn't**.	

Spelling: make → mak**ing**, run → ru**nning**, ti**dy** → ti**dying**

We use the Past Perfect Continuous
• for actions that started in the past and were still in progress when another action started or when something happened.
*I **had been sleeping** for about four hours when the alarm went off.*
• for actions that were in progress in the past and had an effect on a later action.
*Sarah was confident about her exams because she **had been studying** for months.*

> **Note**
> Some common time expressions that are often used with the Past Perfect Continuous are *all day/night/week, for years / a long time / ages, since*. We can use *How long ...?* with the Past Perfect Continuous in questions and *for (very) long* in questions and negative sentences.
> *I'd been trying **all week** to get in touch with Alison.*

Grammar Exercises

2 Circle the correct words.

1 The archeologists **had dug / had been digging** for three months.
2 As soon as I saw his face, I knew he **had won / had been winning** the match.
3 Simon **had tried / had been trying** to find his wallet all morning.
4 They had never **seen / been seeing** such a beautiful painting.
5 After we had **eaten / been eating**, we went out into the garden.
6 How long had you **sat / been sitting** in the waiting room before the doctor saw you?
7 Had you ever **ridden / been riding** a horse before you arrived at Polk Farm?
8 My shoes were dirty because I **had walked / had been walking** in muddy fields.
9 He **hadn't saved / hadn't been saving** money for long, but he already had £50.
10 We **had known / had been knowing** each other for years.

3 Match to form sentences.

1 We had been waiting at the station
2 Tonya was in a bad mood
3 By the time we got to the stadium,
4 As soon as he had got permission to go,
5 Dave and Peter weren't talking to each other
6 They hadn't been on the beach for long
7 I was very excited about Sam's surprise party
8 The kids had been eating sweets all afternoon

a the match had already started.
b before Stella started complaining about the heat.
c for two hours before the train arrived.
d he went.
e because they had been fighting earlier.
f because she hadn't slept well the night before.
g so they weren't hungry by dinner time.
h because I had never been to one before.

4 Complete the sentences with the correct form of the Past Perfect or Past Perfect continuous of the verbs in brackets.

1 By the time I got home last night, everyone _____ (eat) their dinner.
2 We _____ (sail) for most of the afternoon when the weather suddenly changed.
3 The man was angry because he _____ (wait) to be served for nearly an hour.
4 By 1 pm, Stephanie _____ (ride) for six hours, and she was exhausted.
5 I was starving by ten o'clock because I _____ (not have) any breakfast.
6 Until yesterday, the children _____ (never see) a dolphin before.
7 Wendy was pleased because she _____ (find) her perfect job.
8 How long _____ (you / hide) under the bed before Sally finally found you?

5 Choose the correct time expressions to complete the sentences.

1 What had he been doing ___ he hurt himself?
   a before
   b as soon as
   c just
2 ___ I had shut the door, I realised the key was still inside.
   a While
   b As soon as
   c Until
3 They had been working ___ five o'clock in the morning.
   a for
   b when
   c since
4 ___ had the twins been arguing for?
   a What time
   b How long
   c When
5 I had ___ seen the film.
   a yet
   b always
   c already
6 Donna had been looking for a new flat ___ three weeks.
   a for
   b when
   c since
7 They had ___ got to sleep when the phone rang.
   a yet
   b still
   c just
8 He had been climbing for three days, but he ___ hadn't reached the mountain top.
   a yet
   b still
   c just

6 Write questions for the answers using the Past Perfect Simple or the Past Perfect Continuous.

1 _____
   They had been to the museum.
2 _____
   I had warned her three times about her behaviour.
3 _____
   No, he hadn't been invited to the meeting.
4 _____
   I had been trying to phone him for two hours.
5 _____
   I had been sleeping on the sofa.
6 _____
   I had been there twice before.
7 _____
   He had told her last week.
8 _____
   Yes, she had been sunbathing.

Unit 11

7 Read the situations. Then complete the sentences with the Past Perfect or Past Perfect Continuous.

1. He finished his meal. Then he went upstairs to bed.
 After _____, he went upstairs to bed.
2. Sarah got a job in a café. Three weeks later the café closed.
 Sarah _____ for three weeks when it closed.
3. Katy read the book. Then she lent it to me.
 When _____, she lent it to me.
4. The two teams started playing. Ten minutes later it began to snow.
 The two teams _____ when _____.
5. I phoned my mum. Before that I had a guitar lesson.
 I _____ after _____ a guitar lesson.
6. She waited for half an hour. Then she realised she was waiting in the wrong place.
 She _____ before _____.
7. They met in 2010. Then they got married.
 By the time _____, they _____ since 2010.
8. The neighbours' party started at five o'clock. We complained at midnight.
 The neighbours _____ for seven hours when _____.

Vocabulary

Phrasal verbs

8 Match the phrasal verbs with their meanings.

1. set off   a to become extinct or disappear
2. set up   b to leave on a journey
3. take off   c to start to have control of something
4. take over   d to become quickly successful
5. dig up   e to prepare something for use
6. put off   f to tolerate something unpleasant
7. put up with g to remove something from the ground
8. die out   h to discourage

9 Complete the sentences with the correct form of the phrasal verbs from 8.

1. I was _____ the idea of becoming a doctor because somebody told me you have to study for seven years.
2. Can you _____ the computer system for us, please?
3. The dinosaurs _____ before the beginning of the Ice Age.
4. We plan to _____ at around 6 am, which means we'll get there about 11.
5. I don't know how you _____ your little brother's terrible behaviour.
6. When Dad gets tired of driving, Mum usually _____ the wheel for a few hours.
7. Archeologists have _____ some amazing things in the Sahara desert.
8. He invented a new computer game but unfortunately it didn't really _____.

Exam Practice

10 Complete the second sentence so that it has a similar meaning to the first sentence, using the word given. Do not change the word given. You must use between two and five words.

1 After breakfast, we went to the park.
   eaten
   We went to the park _____ breakfast.

2 I got to the party too late to hear the band.
   stopped
   By the time I got to the party _____ playing.

3 She finished using the laptop and then gave it to me.
   soon
   She gave me the laptop _____ finished using it.

4 It was the saddest song I had ever heard.
   never
   I _____ a sadder song.

5 Teddy went to sleep, then his parents came home an hour later.
   sleeping
   Teddy _____ an hour when his parents came home.

6 I don't know how long I can tolerate this hot weather.
   put
   I don't know how long _____ this hot weather.

7 We had no sugar left when we finished cooking.
   used
   By the time we finished cooking, _____ all of the sugar.

8 The departure time for our train is 8.35.
   sets
   Our train _____ 8.35.

11 Choose the correct answers.

1 Nobody ___ seen Mark all day, and they were getting worried about him.
   a have   b had   c has   d having

2 My feet hurt because I had ___ walking for hours.
   a be   b was   c been   d being

3 We went to bed as ___ as we had drunk our hot chocolate.
   a soon   b when   c just   d time

4 I hadn't heard that CD for ___.
   a time   b ages   c far   d never

5 The accident I had last year ___ me off climbing for life.
   a made   b took   c showed   d put

6 My mum has been doing the ironing all ___.
   a time   b long   c since   d morning

7 Who is going to ___ over from you when you leave the company?
   a make   b take   c do   d hold

8 He had been working there ___ 2001.
   a for   b since   c while   d when

Writing

12 Write sentences in your notebook using the Past Perfect Simple and Past Perfect Continuous. Say what you, your family and your friends had done by 2010. What had you/they been doing by that time, and for how long?

By 2010 I had learned to ride a bike / been playing football for five years.

Unit 12

Awareness

1 Which of these sentences are correct (C) and incorrect (I)?

1. Everyone is very excited, isn't he? ___
2. I hope you didn't hurt you. ___
3. Someone has been eating my sandwiches. ___
4. Is this yours torch? ___
5. Nobody told me about that. ___
6. Help yourself to a drink. ___
7. Did they meet anyone when they were away? ___
8. Anything has been done about this yet. ___
9. They love their new house. ___
10. Don't touch that. It's mine! ___

How many did you get right? ☐

Grammar

Question Tags

Question tags are short questions at the end of a positive or negative sentence. They are formed with a modal or an auxiliary verb + a personal pronoun.
We usually use an affirmative question tag after a negative sentence, and a negative question tag after an affirmative sentence.
He's been to Mexico, **hasn't he?**
They can't come tomorrow, **can they?**

When an affirmative sentence contains a verb in the Present Simple or the Past Simple we use *do/does*, *don't/doesn't* and *did/didn't* in the question tag.
You enjoy dancing, **don't you?**
He didn't turn up on time, **did he?**

We use question tags when we want
• someone to agree with what we are saying.
That was a silly thing to do, **wasn't it?**
• to make sure that what we are saying is right.
It's your turn now, **isn't it?**

Remember! Some question tags are irregular. Notice the way these tags are formed.
I'm late, **aren't I?**
Nobody is ill, **are they?**
Let's go on a boat trip, **shall we?**
Don't shout so loud, **will you?**
Look after yourself, **won't you?**
This/That's my seat, **isn't it?**
These/Those are pretty flowers, **aren't they?**

Reflexive Pronouns

Subject Pronoun	Reflexive Pronoun
I	myself
you	yourself
he	himself
she	herself
it	itself
we	ourselves
you	yourselves
they	themselves

We use reflexive pronouns
• when the subject and the object of the sentence are the same.
*I taught **myself** to ride a bike.*
• with some verbs (*behave, blame, cut, enjoy, help, hurt*, etc).
*Don't **blame yourself** – it wasn't your fault.*
• when we want to emphasise that somebody does something alone or without another person's help we often use the word *by*.
*Steve carried the luggage **himself**.*
*She walked home **by herself**.*

Indefinite Pronouns

An indefinite pronoun refers to one or more unspecified people, things or places.
We use *someone, somebody, something* and *somewhere* to talk about an unspecified person, thing or place in affirmative sentences.
***Someone** left their keys in the lock.*
*He must be hiding **somewhere**.*

We use *anyone, anybody, anything* and *anywhere* to talk about an unspecified person, thing or place in negative sentences and questions.
*I can't see **anybody** in the park at the moment.*
*Have you had **anything** to eat?*

We use *everyone, everybody, everything* and *everywhere* to talk about all unspecified people, things or places. They take a singular verb.
***Everyone** loves the new dog.*
*I've seen those posters **everywhere** recently.*

We use *no-one, nobody, nothing* and *nowhere* to talk about no person, thing or place. They have a negative meaning.
***Nobody** spoke to me.*
*There is **nothing** we can do about it.*

Possessive Pronouns

Subject Pronoun	Possessive Adjective	Possessive Pronoun
I	my	mine
you	your	ours
he	his	his
she	her	hers
it	its	-
we	our	ours
you	your	yours
they	their	theirs

We use possessive pronouns to show that something belongs to someone. Possessive pronouns replace a possessive adjective and a noun, or the possessive form and a noun.
*That's **my bag**. It's **mine**.*
*This is **Robin's calculator**. It's **his**.*

Unit 12 67

Unit 12

Grammar Exercises

2 Match the sentences with the question tags.

1. They enjoyed the film,
2. There isn't any cake left,
3. Let's watch the Olympics,
4. You never arrive on time,
5. We'll be alright,
6. He's never enjoyed history,
7. It doesn't look very interesting,
8. I'm your partner,

a won't we?
b does it?
c aren't I?
d has he?
e didn't they?
f shall we?
g is there?
h do you?

3 Add question tags to the following statements.

1. They are going to Pompeii, _____?
2. Be a good boy, _____?
3. Don't forget to phone me, _____?
4. That looks a bit dangerous, _____?
5. These biscuits aren't very nice, _____?
6. She lost her handbag yesterday, _____?
7. I'm getting better, _____?
8. He'll carry my books for me, _____?
9. Let's eat, _____?
10. Nobody's coming, _____?

4 Circle the correct words.

1. Shall I help **you / yourself** with that, or can you do it **you / yourself**?
2. I told **her / herself** she was going to hurt **her / herself**.
3. Did the kids enjoy **them / themselves** yesterday? I haven't seen **them / themselves** since last week.
4. You had better fix **it / itself** soon because it's not going to fix **it / itself**.
5. No, I didn't go to the cinema by **me / myself** – Anna came with **me / myself**.
6. He didn't behave **him / himself**, so they threw **him / himself** out of the team.
7. Please help **you / yourselves** to anything in the fridge. I bought it all for **you / yourselves**.
8. How long had she been looking at **her / herself** in the mirror before her mother called **her / herself**?

5 Complete the text with something, somewhere, someone, anything, anywhere, anyone, everywhere, everyone, nothing, nowhere or no-one.

Dad was feeling sad because (1) _____ had come into Jim's Corner Shop for days. 'Where is (2) _____?' he asked.

'I don't think (3) _____ has got much money to spend,' Mum told him. 'It's the same (4) _____.'

'Well, we have to do (5) _____ to encourage people to come in and buy our things.'

'I know (6) _____ who can help,' Mum replied. That's when she called me.

'What do you want me to do?' I asked. 'I'm only 12! I can't do (7) _____.'

'Sit down, Jack,' said Mum. 'There's (8) _____ to worry about. I just want you to put (9) _____ on and go (10) _____ with it.'

'I don't want to go (11) _____!'

Then mum brought out a big sign and hung it around my neck. The sign said 'COME TO JIM'S CORNER SHOP – (12) _____ IS CHEAPER!'

6 Circle the correct words.
1. I've got a great dog. **Its / Their** name is Rufus.
2. **Our / Ours** house is quite big.
3. This isn't **your / yours** book. It's **my / mine**.
4. I left **my / mine** laptop at home.
5. Tom has forgotten his pen. Can he use **your / yours**?
6. I didn't know Susan was **your / yours** cousin.
7. That bike doesn't belong to me. It's **her / hers**.
8. **Their / Theirs** parents have bought **our / ours** car. It's **their / theirs** now!

7 Choose the correct answers.
1. Don't forget you've got a test tomorrow, ___?
   a have you
   b will you
   c do you
2. ___ wants to speak to you.
   a Anyone
   b Anything
   c Someone
3. There's ___ on TV tonight.
   a nothing
   b nowhere
   c anything
4. Is this magazine ___?
   a yours
   b your
   c you
5. Ouch. I've just cut ___.
   a me
   b my
   c myself
6. Let's go to the theatre tonight, ___?
   a shall we
   b will we
   c don't we
7. I've looked ___ for my wallet, but I can't find it.
   a anywhere
   b somewhere
   c everywhere
8. She blames ___ for what happened.
   a myself
   b herself
   c himself

Vocabulary

Word formation

8 Match the words with their meanings.
1. analyse
2. conclude
3. comedy
4. know
5. proof
6. repeat
7. satisfy
8. theory

a to say or do again
b to make someone happy by giving them what they need
c funny entertainment
d to carefully examine something
e a fact which shows that something is true
f a big complex idea which explains something
g to have certain information
h to decide something after examining or studying it

9 Use the word in capitals to form a word that fits in the gap.
1. I don't like this kind of music – it's too _____. REPEAT
2. It was not _____ that Mr Norris committed the crime. PROVE
3. _____, it was a good idea – but it didn't work in reality. THEORY
4. The scientists did an _____ of the chemicals. ANALYSE
5. Danny is a real _____ – he makes everyone laugh. COMEDY
6. My _____ of the French language is not very good. KNOW
7. I didn't find the meal very _____. SATISFY
8. Did you come to any _____ about this? CONCLUDE

Unit 12 69

Unit 12

Exam Practice

10 Complete the second sentence so that it has a similar meaning to the first sentence, using the word given. Do not change the word given. You must use between two and five words.

1 Please put down that bag – it belongs to me.
   is
   That bag _____, so please put it down.

2 David didn't have any help cooking the dinner this evening.
   himself
   David _____ this evening.

3 I think my pen was stolen.
   someone
   I think _____ pen.

4 I heard that the concert was enjoyed by all the people who went.
   everyone
   I heard _____ the concert.

5 Nothing has been done about the broken window.
   anything
   Nobody _____ about the broken window.

6 Is this notebook yours?
   your
   Is _____ notebook?

7 I hope the children don't misbehave tonight.
   themselves
   I hope _____ tonight.

8 Nobody taught her to play chess.
   herself
   She _____ chess.

11 Complete the sentences with the word that best fits each gap.

1 That car belongs to us. It's _____.
2 You don't want to go home yet, _____ you?
3 I didn't speak to _____ at the party.
4 Laura can't find _____ shoes.
5 Don't come home too late, _____ you?
6 Steve must be hiding _____, but we can't find him.
7 That wasn't very clever, _____ it?
8 I've had no help with this – I had to do it by _____.

Writing

12 Complete these sentences in your notebook so that they are true for you.

1 If I could go anywhere, _____.
2 Something that made me laugh recently was _____.
3 The world would be better if everyone _____.
4 Someone I'd really like to meet is _____.
5 There isn't anywhere I'd rather be than _____.

Review 3

Grammar

1 Circle the correct words to complete the dialogue.

Donna: Katy, are you going into town this afternoon?
Katy: I'm not sure. I **must / might** go if I have time.
Donna: **Could / Shall** you buy me the latest copy of Rock Magazine if you do go?
Katy: OK. But you **must / may** pay me back that £3 you owe me first.
Donna: Oh, I forgot about that. Sorry, I won't **be able to / could** pay you back until tomorrow.
Katy: That's fine. You **mustn't / don't have** to pay me today – but you **mustn't / don't have** forget tomorrow!
Donna: I **won't / don't**.
Katy: You **ought / should** keep a note of how much money you owe people.
Donna: You are right. **Might / Would** you buy me a notebook and pen as well?

2 Complete the sentences with **might have, should have, shouldn't have, can't have, must have, would have** or **needn't have** and the correct form of the verbs in brackets.

1 I _____ (win) the lottery because I never buy a ticket.
2 We're not sure where Jim is – he _____ (go) to the library with Julian.
3 You _____ (buy) that car when you had the chance – you'll never get a better deal.
4 It turned out that we _____ (run) to the station, because the train was 15 minutes late.
5 I'm sure Joel _____ (come) to meet you if you had asked him.
6 Dan _____ (speak) so rudely to that policeman. He's in trouble now!
7 You've finished your dinner already? You _____ (be) very hungry!
8 Where's Brian? He _____ (arrive) by now.

3 Complete the sentences with the correct form of the Past Perfect Simple or Past Perfect Continuous of the verbs in brackets.

1 After we _____ (visit) the Parthenon, we went for lunch.
2 They _____ (walk) in the mountains for about two hours when the thunderstorm began.
3 My feet were sore because I _____ (run).
4 When she _____ (do) all the shopping, she rewarded herself with a cup of coffee.
5 It was obvious that the baby _____ (cry) for quite a long time.
6 He was late because he _____ (not know) that the motorway was closed.
7 The teacher knew when she entered the classroom that the students _____ (not behave) themselves.
8 I was sure I _____ (see) her face somewhere before.

4 Circle the correct words.

1 You **can't / needn't** worry about Fred. He'll be fine.
2 We **had been knowing / had known** for years about our neighbours' problems.
3 Everyone is very tired, **isn't they / aren't they**?
4 I don't know **anybody / nobody** here.
5 Is this coat **you / yours**?
6 You are lucky – you **could / must** have been badly injured.
7 Do we **must / need** to do this test again?
8 How long **had they waited / had they been waiting** before the meal arrived?

Review 3 **71**

Review 3

5 Choose the correct answers.

1. I couldn't find my bag ___.
   a anywhere b nowhere c everywhere
2. Did you hurt ___ when you fell?
   a you b your c yourself
3. Is this yours or is it ___?
   a me b my c mine
4. You can do this, ___?
   a can you b can't you c could you
5. ___ is knocking on the door.
   a Anyone b Someone c Anything
6. The children are playing by ___.
   a themselves b them c theirs
7. That's not his problem, it's ___.
   a her b hers c herself
8. She wouldn't have enjoyed it, ___?
   a would she b will she c wouldn't she
9. We entertained ___ by telling each other stories.
   a us b ours c ourselves
10. Don't tell anyone, ___?
    a do you b won't you c will you

6 Find the mistakes and correct the sentences.

1. You really ought exercise more.

2. Should I told you earlier?

3. We had been standing in line since ten minutes.

4. Don't blame you about it.

5. We forgotten to do our homework.

6. I would asked her if I had the courage.

7. Could you being a bit quieter please?

8. That must have being exciting day!

Exam Practice

7 For questions 1–12, read the text below and think of a word which best fits each gap. Use only one word in each gap. There is an example at the beginning (0).

A costly mistake

In a court of law, the prosecution (0) ___has___ to prove that a person is guilty before he or she can be punished. However, this is not the case if someone is accused (1) _____ doing something wrong outside the legal system.

David Jones and his wife, Paula, were thrilled (2) _____ a friend suggested that David should apply (3) _____ a job in the international company he worked for. He did so, but was puzzled when the company put his interview (4) _____ several times. When he asked his friend (5) _____ this had happened, he got no answer. They wondered what was going (6) _____.

Paula wanted to find out why the company (7) _____ acted this way, so she went to see an uncle who was a policeman. He eventually told her that someone had reported seeing a car with the same registration number (8) _____ her husband's car being driven away (9) _____ the scene of a crime. This information had (10) _____ put on a computer file to which the company had access. At the time of the crime David was abroad, so obviously a mistake had been (11) _____. Nevertheless, the Joneses could not correct the information, and nobody would apologise for (12) _____ error.

8 For questions 13–22, read the text below. Use the word given in capitals at the end of each line to form a word that fits in the gap in the same line. There is an example at the beginning.

Pets care

One of the most surprising (0) ___developments___ in the treatment of patients in   DEVELOP
recent years has been the use of pets. They are not just fun companions, but can play an
important therapeutic role. Pets have been (13) _____ effective in   PROOF
many cases, even those that are considered the most (14) _____.   HOPE
Doctors have reported that patients have shown greater (15) _____ to   DETERMINE
fight their illness. Indeed, with the aid of a pet, the road to (16) _____   RECOVER
is made much smoother. It has been found that young patients can easily build up a
(17) _____ with a dog, cat or rabbit. This makes them feel less   FRIEND
(18) _____ during their stay in hospital. Once a week, a group of   MISERY
(19) _____ staff take the pets to see the patients who learn how   VOLUNTEER
to feed them and handle them (20) _____.   CARE
As a result of several experimental programmes, it is now common
(21) _____ that pets reduce stress. However, it is important   KNOW
that, once such a programme has started, it must be carried through to its conclusion.
If visits are (22) _____, patients do not get better so quickly,   CONTINUE
and in some cases begin to become ill again.

Review 3 **73**

Review 3

Grammar

For questions 1–10, choose the word or phrase that best completes the sentence or conversation.

1. ___ you make some tea, please?
   A Could
   B Did
   C Are
   D May

2. 'Here are some flowers for you.'
   'Oh! You ___ done that!'
   A can't have
   B mustn't have
   C couldn't have
   D shouldn't have

3. 'Why were his eyes so red?'
   'He ___ for eight hours.'
   A had studied
   B had been studying
   C has studied
   D is studying

4. Everyone loves Julia, ___?
   A aren't they
   B doesn't she
   C don't they
   D isn't she

5. 'What's the matter with Tom?'
   'I think he has hurt ___.'
   A him
   B he
   C his
   D himself

6. Did ___ answer when you called?
   A anything
   B anybody
   C somewhere
   D everything

7. 'Did you know where he was?'
   'No, I ___ him since the day before.'
   A hadn't seen
   B haven't seen
   C hadn't been seeing
   D haven't been seeing

8. She ___ work – she's rich!
   A mustn't
   B can't
   C doesn't have to
   D couldn't

9. 'Why did he do such a stupid thing?'
   'He ___ desperate.'
   A should have been
   B must have been
   C can have been
   D needn't have been

10. Be careful, ___ ?
    A aren't you
    B won't you
    C don't you
    D do you

Vocabulary

For questions 11–20, choose the word or phrase that best completes the sentence or conversation.

11. According ___ my calculations, we'll be there at 5.40.
    A at
    B from
    C of
    D to

12. I hope you ___ a success of your new career.
    A do
    B make
    C have
    D get

13. We went out of business because we couldn't make a ___.
    A money
    B price
    C win
    D profit

14. I don't think anybody could ever take John's ___ in this organisation.
    A site
    B place
    C table
    D put

15. You'll never be a success if you don't ___ chances.
    A make
    B hold
    C do
    D take

16. I was going to go, but the weather put me ___.
    A out
    B over
    C up
    D off

17. Many species will ___ out if global warming continues at this rate.
    A go
    B die
    C live
    D exit

18. What time did you set ___ on your journey yesterday?
    A up
    B on
    C off
    D in

19. Do you have any ___ that Mark stole it?
    A knowledge
    B experiment
    C analysis
    D proof

20. I'm so bored by this book. It's too ___.
    A repeating
    B similar
    C repetitive
    D same

Unit 13

Awareness

1 Which of these sentences are correct (C) and incorrect (I)?

1. It's not worth to fight about this. ___
2. I persuaded her going to the café with me. ___
3. She was very happy to hear that you are coming. ___
4. Please don't make me do it all again. ___
5. Were you expecting finish by five o'clock? ___
6. You're not allowed talking during the show. ___
7. I don't remember to see him before. ___
8. Imagine standing by the edge of a volcano! ___
9. It wasn't cold enough to snow on the first day. ___
10. I hope seeing you soon. ___

How many did you get right? ☐

Grammar

Gerunds

We form gerunds with verbs and the *-ing* ending. We can use gerunds
• as nouns.
Drinking too much coffee is bad for you.
• after prepositions.
I'm bored **of waiting**.
• after the verb *go* when we talk about activities.
Tina **goes swimming** every morning.

We also use gerunds after certain verbs and phrases.

admit	(don't) mind	have difficulty	like	risk
avoid	enjoy	imagine	love	spend time
be used to	fancy	involve	miss	suggest
can't help	feel like	it's no good	practise	
can't stand	finish	it's no use	prefer	
deny	forgive	it's (not) worth	prevent	
dislike	hate	keep	regret	

I **don't feel like cooking** tonight.
It's not worth paying someone to repair this old car.

Infinitives

	Active	Passive
Present	(to) send	(to) be sent
Perfect	(to) be sent	(to) have been sent

I'll **clean** your bike.
Your bike **will be cleaned**.
He shouldn't **have sold** his car.
His car shouldn't **have been sold**.

Full Infinitives

We form full infinitives with *to* and the verb. We use full infinitives
• to explain purpose.
I went to the bank **to get** some money.
• after adjectives such as *afraid, scared, happy, glad, pleased, sad,* etc.
I'm **sad to say** the weather is going to stay bad for a while.
• after the words *too* and *enough*.
My head is **too** small **to wear** this hat.
My head isn't big **enough to wear** this hat.

Unit 13 75

Unit 13

We also use full infinitives after certain verbs and phrases.

afford	arrange	expect	invite	offer	pretend	want
agree	ask	fail	learn	persuade	promise	would like
allow	choose	forget	manage	plan	refuse	
appear	decide	hope	need	prepare	seem	

Susan and Marie **refused to get** in the same taxi together.
Would you **like to go** for a walk in the woods?

Bare Infinitives

We use bare infinitives after
- modal verbs.

You **must try** this.
- *had better* to give advice.

You **had better go** and **see** the doctor.
- *would rather* to talk about preference. We often use the word *than*.

She **would rather watch** a film **than read** a book.

Note

1 We use *let* + object + bare infinitive when we want to say that we give permission for someone to do something and it is only used in the active voice. In the passive we can use the verb *to be allowed to*.

The head teacher **let** us all **go** home early that day.
We **were allowed to go** home early that day.

2 We use *make* + object + bare infinitive when we want to say that we force a person to do something in the active voice, but in the passive it's followed by a full infinitive.

My dad **made** me **wash** his car again.
I **was made to wash** Dad's car again.

Gerund or Infinitive?

Some verbs can be followed by a gerund or a full infinitive with no change in meaning. Some common verbs are *begin, bother, continue, hate, like, love* and *start*.
The lady **began to sing/singing** when the curtain went up.
I **hated to go/going** to bed early when I was little.
We didn't **bother to have/having** a shower all weekend.

There are other verbs that can be followed by a gerund or a full infinitive, but the meaning changes. Some common ones are *go on, forget, regret, remember, stop* and *try*.
I **forgot buying** that CD. (I didn't remember that I had bought that CD.)
I **forgot to buy** the CD. (I didn't remember to buy the CD, so I don't have it.)
We **went on walking**. (They continued to walk.)
We **went on to walk** to the border. (They had been walking for a while, then continued walking to the border.)
I **regret not going** to the party. (I didn't go to the party, and now I regret it.)
We **regret to inform** you that the shop is now closed. (We're sorry that we have to tell you this.)
My grandad **remembers seeing** The Beatles. (He saw The Beatles and now he remembers seeing them.)
I **remembered to buy** some milk on the way home today. (I remembered first and then I bought some milk.)
We **stopped playing** because we were tired. (We didn't play any more.)
We **stopped to have** a snack. (We stopped doing something so we could have a snack.)
Try kicking it. (Do it, and see if that works.)
I **tried to kick** it, but I missed. (I made the effort, but didn't succeed.)

Grammar Exercises

2 Circle the correct words.

1. You were very lucky **to survive / surviving** that earthquake!
2. I wouldn't risk **to go / going** out in this weather.
3. The power of nature never fails **amaze / to amaze** me.
4. Why did you refuse **to help / helping** me?
5. The performers went on **to play / playing** through the rain.
6. Do you think we'll be allowed **to visit / visiting** the site of the tornado?
7. Why don't you try **to look / looking** on the Internet for the information?
8. We weren't able to avoid **fall / falling** ill on our trip to India.
9. Did you manage **to get / get** in contact with your friend?
10. It's no use **to cry / crying** – that won't help!

3 Use the prompts to write sentences.

1. I / not interested / make / lots of money

   _____

2. we / not afford / go / on holiday

   _____

3. I / rather / play / chess / than / a computer game

   _____

4. she / regret / not study / harder / when she was at school

   _____

5. Dan / stop / believe / in ghosts / when he was 12

   _____

6. dive / off cliffs / is a dangerous hobby

   _____

7. it / be / kind of you / help / us

   _____

8. you / not need / win every race

   _____

4 Complete the conversation with the correct form of the verbs in brackets.

Interviewer: When did you decide (1) _____ (become) a computer game creator?

Donna: When I don't really know. I've always enjoyed (2) _____ (play) games, but I don't remember (3) _____ (think) 'That's what I want (4) _____ (do) as a job when I'm older.' It just happened.

Interviewer: Was it difficult (5) _____ (get) started in the industry?

Donna: Not for me. I learnt (6) _____ (program) a computer when I was eight and I had spent a lot of time (7) _____ (create) things. So when I saw the job advertised, I expected (8) _____ (get) it. I was very confident!

Interviewer: Would you like (9) _____ (give) some advice to young people who want (10) _____ (work) in the gaming industry?

Donna: You have to (11) _____ (love) computers and be good at (12) _____ (program). Keep (13) _____ (study), and don't give up (14) _____ (try). It's a great job. I'd rather (15) _____ (do) this than anything else in the world!

Unit 13 77

Unit 13

5 Complete the sentences with the correct form of the verbs in brackets.
1. Do you remember _____ (meet) Tony last year?
2. I really regret _____ (not go) to my cousin's wedding.
3. I regret _____ (inform) you that the train has been delayed by 30 minutes.
4. We stopped _____ (get) some lunch before continuing on our journey.
5. It's time you stopped _____ (be) so lazy.
6. After I had read her first book, I went on _____ (read) all of her others.

6 Find the mistakes and correct the sentences where necessary. Put a tick (✓) below those which do not need correcting.
1. I would rather to listen to the news.
2. Try find out what went wrong.
3. We were invited to join the group.
4. It's not worth to spend so much time on this.
5. They tried prevent people selling their tickets on the Internet.
6. She wouldn't let me to cook the dinner.
7. Did you arrange go out with Gary this evening?
8. The hospital continued to admit new patients throughout the day.

7 Complete the sentences with the correct form of **make** or **let**.
1. My mum won't _____ me come out because I have too much homework to do.
2. We were _____ to stay behind after school as a punishment.
3. If you don't want to do it, I won't _____ you. It's your choice.
4. Why do you never _____ the children stay up after nine o'clock? Don't you think they are old enough?
5. Were you _____ to do lots of sports when you were at primary school?
6. Dad _____ me take a shower as soon as I got back from camping. He said I smelled!

Vocabulary

Collocations & Expressions

8 Match to form expressions.
1. to be in deep
2. a ray of
3. as fast as
4. to have your head in the
5. to be down to
6. to feel under the
7. to throw caution to the
8. to go down a

a. weather
b. clouds
c. storm
d. water
e. lightning
f. sunshine
g. earth
h. wind

9 Complete the sentences with the correct form of the expressions from 8.
1 When you do something without caring about the consequences, you _____.
2 If a person is described as _____, they're sensible and practical.
3 When something happens _____, it happens very fast.
4 A _____ is something which makes you feel happier.
5 If you're _____, you're in big trouble.
6 When something _____, it's a huge success with many people.
7 If you feel _____, you're a bit ill.
8 A person with their _____ is not thinking realistically.

Exam Practice

10 Complete the second sentence so that it has a similar meaning to the first sentence, using the word given. Do not change the word given. You must use between two and five words.

1 Mark's parents forbid him to get a tattoo.
   let
   Mark's parents _____ a tattoo.
2 I don't want to go training tonight.
   feel
   I _____ training tonight.
3 'Wash your hands before you eat.' Dad said.
   forget
   Dad told me _____ my hands before I eat.
4 They'd buy it, but they don't have enough money.
   afford
   They _____ it.
5 They forced us to run around the track three times.
   made
   We _____ around the track three times.
6 I stayed in because I wasn't feeling very well.
   weather
   I was _____, so I stayed in.
7 I'm really sorry that I didn't try to help her.
   regret
   I really _____ to help her.
8 The play was a great success last night.
   storm
   The play _____ last night.

11 Complete the sentences with the word that best fits each gap.
1 It's _____ use asking her. She won't help.
2 I'm not _____ to sleeping in such a small bed.
3 He'd rather miss lunch _____ leave the meeting early.
4 Why are you pretending _____ enjoy yourself?
5 I regret _____ volunteering for the army when I was younger.
6 At school, we _____ made to wear a uniform every day.
7 It's _____ remembering that the weather can change any minute.
8 I'd like to _____ some time relaxing on a beach somewhere.

Writing

12 Write a paragraph in your notebook. Write about yourself. Use these words:
be afraid of   be good/terrible at   can't stand   enjoy   would like   would rather ... than ...

Unit 14

Awareness

1 Which of these sentences are correct (C) and incorrect (I)?

1. Today's earthquake was stronger last week's. ___
2. That's the bigest volcano I've ever seen. ___
3. Whales aren't as dangerous as sharks. ___
4. The sooner you finish the best it will be. ___
5. What's the most polluted city in the world? ___
6. We don't have time enough for this. ___
7. It was such a violent storm. ___
8. My dad explained it more clearly than our teacher. ___
9. 5 am is the earlyest I have ever got up in the morning. ___
10. It's too hot to go outside! ___

How many did you get right? ☐

Grammar

Comparison of Adjectives & Adverbs

We use the comparative to compare two people or things. We usually form the comparative by adding *-er* to an adjective or adverb. If the adjective or adverb has two or more syllables, we use the word *more*. We often use the word *than* after the comparative.
DVDs are **more expensive than** CDs.
Today's storm was over **more quickly than** yesterday's.

We use the superlative to compare one person or thing with other people or things of the same type. We usually form the superlative by adding *-est* to the adjective or adverb. If the adjective or adverb has two or more syllables, we use the word *most*. We use the word *the* before the superlative.
What is **the highest** volcano in the world?
Julian played **the most skillfully**.

Spelling: hot ➜ hot**ter**/hot**test**, brave ➜ brav**er**/brav**est**, tiny ➜ tin**ier**/tin**iest**

Some adjectives and adverbs are irregular and form their comparative and superlative in different ways.

Adjective/Adverb	Comparative	Superlative
good/well	better	the best
bad/badly	worse	the worst
many/more	more	the most
much	more	the most
little	less	the least
far	farther/further	the farthest/furthest

> **Note**
> 1. Some words like *hard, late, straight* and *fast* are both adjectives and adverbs.
> 2. Other words *friendly, lovely, silly,* and *ugly*, even though they end in *-ly* are not adverbs but adjectives.
> 3. The words *hardly* (= barely) and *lately* (= recently) are not the adverbs of *hard* and *late*.

Other comparative structures

We use *as* + adjective/adverb + *as* to show that two people or things are similar in some way.
Do you think the USA is **as big as** China?

We use *not as/so* + adjective/adverb + *as* to show that one person or thing has less of a quality than another.
Mark isn't **as fast as** Mary.

We use *the more/less* + comparative, *the more/less* + comparative to show how one action or situation affects another.
The colder the weather, **the higher** the risk of ice.

80

Too, Enough, So & Such

We use *too* + adjective/adverb to show that something is more than we want or need.
It's **too far** to walk.
He was running **too quickly** for me to catch him.

We use adjective/adverb + *enough* or *enough* + noun to show that something is or isn't as much as we want or need.
You weren't trying **hard enough**.
We have **enough lemonade** for everyone.

We use *so* and *such* for emphasis. It is stronger than *very*.
• We use *so* + adjective/adverb.
The boy's face was **so dirty**!
• We use *such* + (adjective) + noun.
The house was in **such bad condition**.

Note

We can also use *so* and *such* to emphasise characteristics that lead to a certain result or action.
He is **such a funny comedian** that I never miss one of his shows.
The film was **so boring** that we all fell asleep.

Grammar Exercises

2 Circle the correct words.

1 She's the **most nice / nicest** person I have ever met.
2 We didn't get there as **quick / quickly** as we wanted to.
3 The **warm / warmer** the water, the more pleasant the swim.
4 You can't play as **good / well** as I do.
5 That was the **worse / worst** song I have ever heard.
6 Do you know the **higher / highest** mountain in the world?
7 Cats are **more clever / cleverer** than dogs.
8 Storms happen **more frequently / frequenter** in the summer.

3 Complete the dialogues with the comparative or superlative form of the adjectives in brackets.

A Tom: What's your favourite subject? I think maths is (1) _____ (good).
Laura: Are you serious? Maths is (2) _____ (bad) subject in school. Even geography is (3) _____ (interesting) than maths – and I think geography is boring!
Tom: So, what do you like?
Laura: For me, history is (4) _____ (interesting) subject.

B Sue: Wow. That was (5) _____ (funny) film I've ever seen!
Jake: Do you think so? I think the first one was (6) _____ (funny) than that one.
Sue: I haven't seen the first one yet.
Jake: You'll love it. I have never laughed (7) _____ (loud) in my life!
Sue: Was it (8) _____ (exciting) than that one as well?
Jake: Yes, it was just a much (9) _____ (good) film.

Unit 14   81

Unit 14

4 Rewrite the sentences using (not) as ... as.

1. The red bike is cheaper than the blue one.
   The blue bike isn't _____.
2. Earthquakes are scarier than thunderstorms.
   Thunderstorms aren't _____.
3. Paris and London are equally polluted.
   London is _____.
4. Donna speaks more clearly than Carla.
   Carla doesn't _____.
5. You and I play the guitar equally well.
   I play the guitar _____.
6. He drives much faster than she does.
   She doesn't _____.
7. My mum is taller than my dad.
   My dad isn't _____.
8. My brother and my sister are equally clever.
   My sister is _____.

5 Rewrite the sentences with the + comparative, the + comparative.

1. As it got darker, it got colder.
   The _darker it got, the colder it got_ .
2. You will live longer if you are healthy.
   The _____.
3. As the man got closer, we became more nervous.
   The closer _____.
4. If you study harder, you'll know more.
   The harder _____.
5. As he gets older, his hair gets greyer.
   The _____.
6. If they play their music loudly, the neighbours will get angry.
   The louder _____.
7. As the weather gets warmer, people become happier.
   The _____.
8. As I work hard, I get tired.
   The _____.

6 Complete the sentences with too or enough.

1. This coffee isn't hot _____.
2. This tea is _____ cold.
3. He is tall _____ to reach the shelf.
4. It's much _____ hot to sit in the garden.
5. Are you old _____ to drive?
6. No, I'm _____ young to drive.
7. We were _____ afraid to go outside.
8. There wasn't _____ time to finish our meal.
9. Don't be _____ late tonight.
10. We'll catch the first bus if we get up early _____.

82

7 Complete the sentences with so or such.

1 That was _____ an amazing film.
2 It was _____ a small earthquake that hardly anyone noticed it.
3 He talks _____ quickly that nobody can understand him.
4 The storm began _____ suddenly that we all got wet.
5 It's _____ a beautiful day!
6 Your house is _____ lovely.
7 My uncle tells _____ boring stories.
8 I've never seen _____ a tiny computer.

Vocabulary

Prepositions

8 Complete the phrases with these prepositions. You will need to use some prepositions more than once.

by   from   on

1 to do research   _____
2 to drop   _____
3 to live   _____
4 to prevent   _____
5 to be surprised   _____
6 to be different   _____
7 to hold something   _____
8 to recover   _____

9 Complete the sentences with the correct form of the phrases from 8.

1 I don't know why I'm so _____ my brother. We're nearly the same age.
2 We _____ the dog _____ its collar until the owner arrived.
3 The fence is to _____ animals _____ leaving the field.
4 Have you done much _____ climate change?
5 I can't wait to play tennis again after I _____ this knee injury.
6 The price of houses has _____ 10% in the last year.
7 We were _____ the eruption of the volcano – nobody was expecting it.
8 Koala bears _____ the leaves of one particular tree.

Unit 14 83

Unit 14

Exam Practice

10 Complete the second sentence so that it has a similar meaning to the first sentence, using the word given. Do not change the word given. You must use between two and five words.

1 Tanya and Sylvia are the same age.
   old
   Sylvia _____ Tanya.

2 You can't go out at night because you are too young.
   old
   You _____ to go out at night.

3 Nobody in the school dances better than Marco.
   the
   Marco _____ in the school.

4 The storm was so violent that our windows were broken.
   such
   It was _____ that our windows were broken.

5 I thought the test would be harder.
   hard
   The test _____ I expected.

6 Our hands and feet hurt because of the cold.
   so
   It _____ that our hands and feet hurt.

7 As our cat grows older, it gets fatter.
   the
   The older our cat grows, _____ gets.

8 We are too poor to go on holiday this year.
   rich
   We aren't _____ on holiday this year.

11 Use the word in capitals to form a word that fits in the gap.

1 It was the most _____ earthquake the country had ever suffered. **DESTROY**
2 The village was evacuated before the _____. **ERUPT**
3 A _____ event was responsible for the extinction of the dinosaurs. **CATASTROPHE**
4 A _____ tsunami destroyed half the town. **MASS**
5 _____, there were no survivors. **FORTUNATE**
6 The minotaur is a _____ beast. **MYTH**
7 The second eruption was much greater in _____ than the first. **INTENSE**
8 We had been vaccinated, and so were _____ to the disease. **RESIST**

Writing

12 Write a paragraph in your notebook. Write about some of your friends and family. Use comparative and superlative forms of some of these adjectives:

boring   clever   emotional   funny   good   happy   short   sporty   tall

Awareness

1 Which of these sentences are correct (C) and incorrect (I)?

1. The window was broke with a stone. ___
2. The film will be being produced next year. ___
3. Are you being interviewed at lunchtime? ___
4. We were showed the painting by the owner. ___
5. This must be finished by tomorrow. ___
6. What will be done about it? ___
7. The news were broadcast at 9 pm. ___
8. They'll be being given some more homework. ___
9. This program is been shown all over the world. ___
10. This room needs to be cleaned. ___

How many did you get right? ☐

Grammar
Passive voice: Tenses

We use the passive when
- the action is more important than who or what is responsible for it (the agent).

*A thief **was arrested** yesterday.*

- we don't know the agent, or it is not important.

*The film **will be released** in over a thousand cinemas.*

> **Note**
> When it is important to mention the agent in a passive sentence, we use the word *by*. When we want to mention a tool or material in the passive sentence, we use the word *with*.
>
> *A journalist **interviewed** me.*
> *I **was interviewed by** a journalist.*
> *The plates **were smashed with** a hammer.*

The passive is formed with the verb *be* and a past participle. Notice how the active verb forms change to passive verb forms.

Tense	Active	Passive
Present Simple	take/takes	am/are/is taken
Present Continuous	am/are/is taking	am/are/is being taken
Past Simple	took	was/were taken
Past Continuous	was/were taking	was/were being taken
Present Perfect	have/has taken	have/has been taken
Past Perfect Simple	had taken	had been taken
Future Simple	will take	will be taken

> **Note**
> There is no passive form for Future Continuous, Present Perfect Continuous and Past Perfect Continuous.

We change an active sentence into a passive sentence in the following way:

The object of the verb in the active sentence becomes the subject of the verb in the passive sentence. The verb *be* is used in the same tense of the main verb in the active sentence, together with the past participle of the main verb in the active sentence.
*They **were filming** her. She **was being filmed**.*

In this example we do not know who was filming her and it is not very important, so we do not include this information in the passive sentence.

Unit 15

> **Note**
>
> When we want to change an active sentence with two objects into the passive voice, one becomes the subject of the passive sentence and the other one remains an object. Which object we choose depends on what we want to emphasise. If the personal object remains an object in the passive sentence, then we have to use a suitable preposition (*to, for*, etc).
>
> I showed **her the camera**.
> She **was shown** the camera.
> The camera **was shown to** her.

Passive Voice: Gerunds, Infinitives & Modal Verbs

	Active	Passive
Gerund	taking	being taken
Bare infinitive	take	be taken
Full infinitive	to take	to be taken
Modal	can take	can be taken

Nobody likes **being told** what to do.
The filming **had better be finished** before dark.
He agreed **to be photographed**.
All scripts **must be** carefully **checked** before they are given to the actors.

Grammar Exercises

2 Circle the correct words.

1 The show is **been / being** recorded at the moment.
2 My novel has been **made / making** into a film.
3 Your essay needs **being / to be** edited more carefully.
4 You **will given / will be given** a prize if you win.
5 Where was this photo **taken / took**?
6 I would like my work to be **read / reading** by everyone.
7 You can't do that! It **isn't / doesn't** allowed.
8 This had better **be / being** cleaned by tomorrow afternoon.
9 Where **are / is** most computer games produced?
10 Have you been **taught / teaching** how to use this camera?

3 Put the sentences into the passive.

1 They make films.   Films _____.
2 They are making a film. A film _____.
3 They made a film.   _____
4 They were making a film. _____
5 They have made a film.   _____
6 They had made a film.   _____
7 They will make a film.   _____
8 They are going to make a film. _____
9 They will have made a film.   _____

4 Rewrite the sentences in the passive.

1. Spectators mustn't throw anything onto the stage.
   Nothing must be thrown onto the stage.
2. Someone needs to fix this.
   This _____.
3. They are making a lot of noise.
   A lot of noise _____.
4. Nobody can do it.
   It _____.
5. People will remember her forever.
   She _____.
6. Somebody might have stolen the bag.
   The bag _____.
7. They should arrest him.
   He _____.
8. You have to switch it off.
   It _____.

5 Rewrite the sentences in the passive.

1. Somebody had broken the TV.

2. Simon will interview the actor.

3. They have found a cure for the disease!

4. They close the café at 5 pm.

5. A million people watched the show.

6. They will have found him by now.

7. Someone ought to feed this dog.

8. A person is reviewing the film.

6 Use the prompts to write questions in the passive.

1. wine / produce / in the UK

2. the 2012 Olympics / hold / in London

3. send / a man to Mars / by 2020

4. Harry Potter / write / by J.K. Rowling

5. coffee / grow / in Iceland

6. Where / Mercedes cars / make

Unit 15

7 Complete the sentences with the correct form, active or passive, of the verbs in brackets.

1. My dad _____ (take) that photo of me, and it _____ (frame) by my uncle.
2. **A:** '_____ mobile phones _____ (can / use) on this plane?'
   B: 'No, but you _____ (can / use) your laptop.'
3. I'm sure the trophy _____ (win) by a South American team next year.
4. **A:** 'She _____ (fix) her bike just now. She can't come to the phone.'
   B: '_____ (you / ask) her to phone me, please?'
5. **A:** 'This video _____ (download) half a million times so far this year.'
   B: 'I _____ (not see) it yet.'
6. Your homework _____ (must / complete) by Friday, and it _____ (should / print) on good quality paper.
7. Last night we _____ (make) some pizzas, and they _____ (eat) very quickly.
8. Tomorrow, I _____ (take) the car to the garage, where it _____ (repair).

Vocabulary

Phrasal verbs

8 Match the phrasal verbs with their meanings.

1	bring out	a	to collect someone or something and take them somewhere
2	bring round	b	to publish
3	pick out	c	to stop paying attention to something
4	pick up	d	to convince someone that your point of view is correct
5	ring back	e	to phone a TV or radio station
6	ring in	f	to choose
7	tune in	g	to return a phone call
8	tune out	h	to choose a particular radio station

9 Complete the sentences with the correct form of the phrasal verbs from 8.

1. He didn't agree with me at first, but I _____ him _____ eventually.
2. I _____ to Radio 4 last night and heard a very funny play.
3. What time are you going to _____ me _____ to take me to school tomorrow?
4. I can't talk just now – can I _____ you _____ later?
5. They say she is going to _____ a new book in the winter.
6. It was such a boring lecture that I _____ after ten minutes.
7. Will you come shopping with me tomorrow to help me _____ a new pair of shoes?
8. Listeners are encouraged to _____ to the station and speak to the DJ.

Exam Practice

10 Complete the second sentence so that it has a similar meaning to the first sentence, using the word given. Do not change the word given. You must use between two and five words.

1 They weren't giving the children any attention.
   given
   The children _____ any attention.

2 You have to clean this house now.
   has
   This house _____ now.

3 Did your mum make this cake?
   by
   Was _____ your mum?

4 Shane plays a very important role in this production.
   played
   A very important role _____ in this production.

5 They might build a new sports centre in town.
   built
   A new sports centre _____ in town.

6 I told you not to do that.
   were
   You _____ that.

7 I stopped concentrating halfway through the lesson.
   tuned
   I _____ halfway through the lesson.

8 They chose some nice clothes for me to wear.
   picked
   Some nice clothes _____ for me to wear.

11 Choose the correct answers.

1 How many of these __ made every year?
   a are   b be   c do   d done

2 My shirt was designed __ Giorgio Armani.
   a with   b on   c by   d on

3 Gina was __ interviewed by a TV reporter.
   a in   b be   c doing   d being

4 All accidents __ be reported immediately.
   a are   b need   c must   d have

5 I'll __ you up at 7.20.
   a pick   b put   c make   d have

6 This meat __ to be cooked a little bit longer.
   a might   b must   c ought   d may

7 I can't help tuning __ when I'm bored by something.
   a out   b up   c in   d over

8 When we arrived, we __ shown to our rooms by the manager.
   a are   b were   c was   d did

Speaking

12 Write five quiz questions in the passive in your notebook. Ask the class your questions. How many did they get right?

When were the London Olympics held?

Unit 16

Awareness

1 Which of these sentences are correct (C) and incorrect (I)?

1. He is say to be the best singer of his generation. ___
2. It is thought that mobile phones can cause cancer. ___
3. The new sports centre said to be fantastic. ___
4. It is expect that the plane will arrive on time. ___
5. This city is considered being the safest in the world. ___
6. Marco is supposed to be an excellent tennis player. ___
7. It is known that global temperatures are rising. ___
8. That newspaper knows to be inaccurate. ___
9. Your brother is expected to do well in this race. ___
10. It is considered rude to leave the table without permission. ___

How many did you get right? ☐

Grammar

Passive voice: Impersonal & Personal structures

We often use verbs like *believe, consider, know, expect, say, suppose* and *think* in the passive voice. They can be used in an impersonal or a personal passive structure.

We form the impersonal passive structure with *it* + passive verb + *that* + clause.
Many people believe that the BBC is the best news source.
It is believed that the BBC is the best news source.

We form the personal structure with noun + passive verb + full infinitive.
Many people say that the Internet has changed the way we think.
The Internet is said to have changed the way we think.

Grammar Exercises

2 Use the prompts to write sentences.

1. said / this film / boring / is / to be
   _____

2. that / chimpanzees / believed / can use language / it / is
   _____

3. supposed / Carla's essay / very good / to be / is
   _____

4. digital cameras / said / getting cheaper / are / to be
   _____

5. that / thought / is / radio / is becoming / less popular / it
   _____

6. considered / his best / his latest book / to be / is
   _____

7. said / the company / is doing / very well / is / it / that
   _____

8. haunted / that house / to be / believed / is
   _____

3 Rewrite the sentences.

1 They say she is responsible for all the problems.   It _____.
2 People think that pirates kidnapped the family.   It _____.
3 They say that he is going to sell his business.   It _____.
4 People believe that life exists on other planets.   It _____.
5 They know that the ring was stolen during the war.   It _____.
6 They say that he trains harder than anyone.   It _____.
7 People believe that black cats are lucky.   It _____.
8 They say that Simon is a great guitarist.   It _____.

4 Rewrite the sentences in 3 using the personal passive structure.

1 She is said to be responsible for all the problems.
2 _____
3 _____
4 _____
5 _____
6 _____
7 _____
8 _____

5 Rewrite the sentences.

1 People think this government is useless.
  a It _is thought that this government is useless_____.
  b This _government is thought to be useless_____.
2 They believed that the man was guilty.
  a It _____.
  b The man _____.
3 People expect Graham to be very successful.
  a It _____.
  b Graham _____.
4 They think that there is gold under those hills.
  a It _____.
  b Gold _____.
5 People believed that the earth was flat.
  a It _____.
  b The earth _____.
6 People understand that nurses work very hard.
  a It _____.
  b Nurses _____.
7 They think that the volcano is about to erupt.
  a It _____.
  b The volcano _____.
8 They say Sharon is the best photographer in the school.
  a It _____.
  b Sharon _____.

Unit 16

6 Find the mistakes and correct the sentences.

1 The criminal said to be hiding in France.
_____

2 He is said that TV is damaging family life.
_____

3 They are thought looking for a new home.
_____

4 It is consider rude to speak with your mouth full.
_____

5 Documentaries is said to be educational.
_____

6 It is known that life evolve on earth.
_____

7 This TV drama is expecting to win lots of awards.
_____

7 Complete the sentences with the word that best fits each gap.

1 _____ is thought that nuclear power is the answer to our energy problems.
2 Yamaha motorcycles _____ considered to be the fastest in the world.
3 It _____ said that they are the worst team in the league.
4 My father is believed to _____ a very important man.
5 It is expected _____ the economy will grow a little next year.
6 Too much exercise is considered _____ be bad for you.
7 His plan was thought to be _____ silly one.
8 She is believed to be _____ greatest painter of her generation.

Vocabulary

Word formation

8 Match the words with their meanings.

1 act   a a picture taken with a camera
2 adventure   b a magazine about a particular subject
3 journal   c to do something
4 photo   d ideas about how to govern a country
5 politics   e normal
6 risk   f an exciting experience
7 satisfy   g to make someone happy giving them what they need
8 usual   h the possibility of something bad happening

9 Use the word in capitals to form a word that fits in the gap.

1 Daniel is training to be a _____.   JOURNAL
2 Where is Becky? It is very _____ for her to be late for anything.   USUAL
3 It's _____ to ride in the city without a helmet.   RISK
4 That meal was rather _____, because there was not enough of it.   SATISFY
5 I love films with plenty of _____ and special effects.   ACT
6 Stephan is a very _____ type of person, isn't he?   ADVENTURE
7 My brother wants to be a _____ when he grows up.   POLITICS
8 _____ is a much more popular hobby than it was twenty years ago.   PHOTO

Exam Practice

10 Complete the second sentence so that it has a similar meaning to the first sentence, using the word given. Do not change the word given. You must use between two and five words.

1 Experts believe that there is life on Mars.
 believed
 It _____ there is life on Mars.

2 They say that Julia plays the piano very well.
 to
 Julia _____ the piano very well.

3 People know the moon is not made of cheese.
 be
 The moon _____ made of cheese.

4 People think Melanie is afraid of mice.
 is
 It _____ is afraid of mice.

5 They say they are going to build a new library.
 said
 It _____ a new library is going to be built.

6 People expect Johnny Depp to win the prize.
 expected
 Johnny Depp _____ win the prize.

7 They allowed us to swim in the sea.
 were
 We _____ in the sea.

8 They have just reported that the game is over.
 been
 It _____ that the game is over.

11 Choose the correct answers.

1 Samantha is ___ to be an excellent dancer.
 a told b said c spoken d heard

2 It is ___ good manners to say 'Thank you' after a meal.
 a known b expected c considered d said

3 We ___ believed to be terrorists by the police.
 a were b was c am d had

4 ___ was believed that the sun orbited the earth.
 a He b We c They d It

5 Some people consider television to ___ a terrible invention.
 a make b be c do d live

6 It ___ known that smoking is very bad for your health.
 a are b has c does d is

7 Maria is ___ to be living in Spain now.
 a believed b hoping c knowing d better

8 We were ___ to visit the hospital between 1 pm and 3 pm.
 a let b allowed c could d might

Writing

12 Write six sentences in your notebook using the impersonal and personal passive structure. Use these ideas to help you.

- Something that is believed to be true.
- Something that is known to be false.
- Something or someone that is considered to be the best at something.
- Something or someone that is thought to be funny.
- Something that is often said.

Unit 16 93

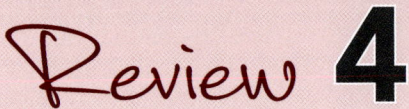

Grammar

1 Complete the text with the correct form of the verbs in brackets.

My name is Natasha. I'm 13 years old, and I want **(1)** _____ (be) an Olympic athlete. I enjoy **(2)** _____ (run) and **(3)** _____ (jump), but the event I would like **(4)** _____ (become) champion at is the javelin. I'm very lucky **(5)** _____ (have) a great coach. He makes me **(6)** _____ (train) really hard every day, and expects me **(7)** _____ (do) my best all the time. We spend a lot of time **(8)** _____ (practise) after school and at weekends, too. Sometimes it is hard **(9)** _____ (get) up early on Saturday and Sunday mornings. Often I feel like **(10)** _____ (stay) in bed all day, but it's no use **(11)** _____ (complain). My coach refuses **(12)** _____ (let) me give up. I don't mind **(13)** _____ (do) what he tells me – because he is my dad!

2 Complete the sentences with the comparative or superlative form of the adjectives in brackets.

1. That was _____ (good) football match ever!
2. Geography is _____ (interesting) than maths.
3. Steve is _____ (bad) player on the team.
4. I don't want to walk _____ (far) than the bus stop.
5. Who has _____ (big) bike?
6. Marie is much _____ (nice) than Stephan.
7. That's _____ (ridiculous) thing I have ever heard.
8. A hippopotamus is _____ (dangerous) than an elephant.

3 Rewrite the sentences in the passive.

1. Someone needs to wash the car.
   The car _____.
2. People will never forget him.
   He _____.
3. They are catching a lot of fish.
   A lot of fish _____.
4. They teach computer science at this college.
   Computer science _____.
5. You have to feed it twice a day.
   It _____.
6. They should send her to a different school.
   She _____.
7. Someone gave me directions.
   I _____.
8. Nobody said anything about the problem.
   Nothing _____.

4 Rewrite the sentences in two ways.
1. People think aliens built the pyramids.
   a It _____.
   b Aliens _____.
2. They say that computers have made life easier.
   a It _____.
   b Computers _____.
3. People believe that ghosts exist.
   a It _____.
   b Ghosts _____.
4. They know that the burglar is a woman.
   a It _____.
   b The burglar _____.
5. People say that Greg is able to speak five languages.
   a It _____.
   b Greg _____.
6. They say horse riding is the most dangerous sport.
   a It _____.
   b Horse riding _____.

5 Circle the correct words.
1. It's hard to avoid **making / to make** mistakes.
2. She refused **saying / to say** anything about the test.
3. What is the **better / best** book you have ever read?
4. This cake is not as tasty **as / like** the last one you made.
5. The computer lab was **equip / equipped** with the latest technology.
6. **It / He** is thought that the universe is 14 billion years old.
7. Why did he deny **to be / being** paid the money?
8. Martha is said **to have / having** the loudest voice in the class.

6 Find the mistakes and correct the sentences.
1. She is believed that working in television is very enjoyable.
   _____
2. My guitar was broke by my little brother.
   _____
3. The quicker you run, the most likely you are to win.
   _____
4. You are not as clever like Jonathan.
   _____
5. Oh no! I forgot switching off the cooker.
   _____
6. You had better to give that back to Tom.
   _____
7. Nature documentaries are said being very expensive to make.
   _____
8. That's the most funny joke I've ever heard.
   _____

Review 4 95

Review 4

Exam Practice

7 For questions 1–12, read the text below and decide which answer (A, B, C or D) best fits each gap. There is an example at the beginning (0).

A young contender

(0) ___, bowls is described as being a (1) ___ which is played by senior citizens, so the announcement that a ten year old will be taking (2) ___ in the National Bowls Championship has come as a shock to many players.

At the age of five, Ean Morton (3) ___ his football boots for a set of bowls which once (4) ___ to his great grandmother. He (5) ___ to bowls at once but it can't have been easy for Ean because he (6) ___ to play against people who could take (7) ___ of his inexperience. In spite of the fact that Ean did not achieve (8) ___ success at bowls, he refused to allow it to (9) ___ his enjoyment of it. He continued to practise and enjoy the game.

Now, five years later, Ean is more than a match for most of his opponents. He is very excited (10) ___ playing in the tournament but admits that he doesn't really (11) ___ what to expect. His father, who will also be playing in the championship, is more optimistic. He believes that Ean will reach the top and is prepared to (12) ___ by him every step of the way.

0	A	conservatively	B	traditionally	C	customarily	D	practically
1	A	match	B	contest	C	game	D	tournament
2	A	play	B	bit	C	piece	D	part
3	A	swapped	B	converted	C	switched	D	bartered
4	A	owned	B	belonged	C	possessed	D	effected
5	A	liked	B	stood	C	set	D	took
6	A	must	B	had	C	ought	D	would
7	A	benefit	B	advantage	C	profit	D	gain
8	A	sudden	B	straight	C	direct	D	instant
9	A	spoil	B	rot	C	stain	D	damage
10	A	for	B	from	C	about	D	with
11	A	know	B	realise	C	recognise	D	understand
12	A	support	B	set	C	stand	D	back

(Example answer: 0 B traditionally)

8 For questions 13–24, read the text below and think of the word which best fits each gap. Use only one word in each gap. There is an example at the beginning (0).

Bamboo

Bamboos are the (0) __fastest__ growing plants in the world. Even in countries like England, (13) _____ the plant does not grow naturally, it is known to be capable (14) _____ increasing in height by 15 centimetres in just 24 hours.

Such rapid growth is necessary because the plant has only 8–12 weeks before the dry weather sets (15) _____ to go from ground level to its maximum height, (16) _____ may be as much as 15 metres.

Bamboos are quite demanding. Not (17) _____ do they need a great deal of water in (18) _____ to grow so quickly, but they also need deep soil (19) _____ that their roots can stay warm at colder times of the year. This means the gardener must make sure the ground is not (20) _____ stony for the plant to grow on.

(21) _____ bamboos used to be quite rare in British gardens, they have recently gained popularity with British gardeners. This is because they are green all the year round, (22) _____ are no insects in Britain which destroy them (23) _____ they can grow so close together that not even a cat is thin (24) _____ to squeeze through.

96

Grammar

9 For questions 1–10, choose the word or phrase that best completes the sentence or conversation.

1 You promised ___ me to the show tonight!
  A take
  B taking
  C to take
  D taken

2 'You're home very late tonight!'
  'I know. The teacher wouldn't let us ___ !'
  A leave
  B leaving
  C to leave
  D left

3 'What did you think of the lesson?'
  'I've been to ___ ones than that.'
  A much interesting
  B most interesting
  C the most interesting
  D more interesting

4 The nearer the time comes, ___ I get.
  A more anxious
  B the more anxious
  C most anxious
  D the most anxious

5 How many people is this newspaper ___?
  A read with
  B reading with
  C read by
  D reading by

6 This medicine should only ___ to your dog.
  A give
  B be give
  C given
  D be given

7 'Who is going to win this match?'
  'Daniel ___ the favourite.'
  A is said to be
  B is saying to be
  C is said being
  D says being

8 I can't let you in. You aren't ___ .
  A too old
  B old enough
  C enough old
  D too young

9 The film was ___ that I couldn't sleep that night.
  A so scary
  B scary so
  C such scary
  D such a scary

10 I didn't remember ___ my umbrella.
  A to brought
  B to bringing
  C bringing
  D to bring

Vocabulary

10 For questions 11–20, choose the word or phrase that best completes the sentence.

11 You'll be in ___ water if you're late for work again.
  A cold
  B blue
  C deep
  D rough

12 My band is ___ out its first CD next week.
  A bringing
  B making
  C showing
  D publishing

13 We have done a lot of research ___ this subject.
  A off
  B of
  C over
  D on

14 Sally has got her ___ in the clouds.
  A face
  B head
  C hair
  D eyes

15 Can you help me ___ out a tie to match this shirt?
  A make
  B pick
  C choose
  D take

16 He is very different ___ his father.
  A from
  B against
  C off
  D compared

17 Let's ___ caution to the wind!
  A kick
  B push
  C slap
  D throw

18 I tuned ___ halfway through the boring documentary.
  A up
  B on
  C off
  D out

19 Mario is feeling a bit under the ___ today.
  A clouds
  B sun
  C weather
  D sky

20 My joke went down a ___ with the whole class.
  A lightning
  B wind
  C volcano
  D storm

Review 4

Unit 17

Awareness

1 Which of these sentences are correct (C) and incorrect (I)?

1. She said that she liked computers. ___
2. My teacher told I to be quiet. ___
3. He asked did I wanted to eat something. ___
4. I told I had been working all day. ___
5. What did he say you? ___
6. She asked me when I had made my decision. ___
7. They asked us if we liked football? ___
8. You said that you weren't coming. ___
9. He said me he was reading. ___
10. Tom told me he would fix it. ___

How many did you get right? ☐

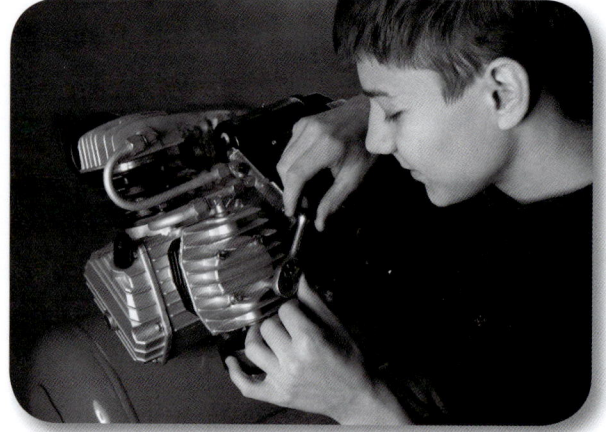

Grammar

Reported Speech: Statements

When we report direct speech, the tenses used by the speaker usually change as follows:

Present Simple	Past Simple
'He **enjoys** dancing,' she said.	She said (that) he **enjoyed** dancing.
Present Continuous	Past Continuous
'She **is studying** chemistry,' he said.	He said (that) she **was studying** chemistry.
Present Perfect Simple	Past Perfect Simple
'They **have passed** their exams,' she said.	She said (that) they **had passed** their exams.
Present Perfect Continuous	Past Perfect Continuous
'They **have been looking** for games,' she said.	She said (that) they **had been looking** for games.
Past Simple	Past Perfect Simple
'She **went** to a show,' he said.	He said (that) she **had gone** to a show.
Past Continuous	Past Perfect Continuous
'He **was listening** to music,' she said.	She said (that) he **had been listening** to music.

Other changes in verb forms are as follows:

can	could
'He **can** play the trumpet,' she said.	She said (that) he **could** play the trumpet.
may	might
'He **may** be late,' she said.	She said (that) he **might** be late.
must	had to
'He **must** go to bed,' she said.	She said (that) he **had to** go to bed.
will	would
'They **will go** to France,' she said.	She said (that) they **would go** to France.

> **Note**
>
> 1. We often use the verbs *say* and *tell* in reported speech. We follow *tell* with an object.
>   *My teacher **said** I should study more.* ➜ *My teacher **told me** that I should study more.*
> 2. We can leave out *that*.
>   *He **said that** he preferred English.* ➜ *He **said** he preferred English.*
> 3. Remember to change pronouns and possessive adjectives where necessary.
>   '**We** are watching TV,' he said. ➜ *He said (that) **they** were watching TV.*
>   '*That's **my** bag,*' she said. ➜ *She said (that) that was **her** bag.*
> 4. The following tenses and words don't change in Reported Speech: Past Perfect Simple, Past Perfect Continuous, *would, could, might, should, ought to, used to, had better, mustn't* and *must* when they refer to deduction.

Reported Speech: Changes in Time & Place

When we report direct speech, there are often changes in words that show time and place too.

now	then
'I'm resting **now**,' she said.	She said she was resting **then**.
today	that day
'They're staying at home **today**,' he said.	He said they were staying at home **that day**.
tonight	that night
'I want to see a film **tonight**,' she said.	She said she wanted to see a film **that night**.
yesterday	the previous day / the day before
'I wasn't well **yesterday**,' he said.	He said he hadn't been well **the previous day / the day before**.
last week/month	the previous week/month / the week/month before
'He left work **last month**,' she said.	She said he had left work **the previous month / the month before**.
tomorrow	the next day / the following day
'We'll go to the cinema **tomorrow**,' she said.	She said they would go to the cinema **the next day / the following day**.
next week/month	the following week/month
'I'm starting piano lessons **next week**,' she said.	She said she was starting piano lessons **the following week**.
this/these	that/those
'**This** is my car,' she said.	She said **that** was her car.
ago	before
'The race started two hours **ago**,' she said.	She said the race had started two hours **before**.
at the moment	at that moment
'He's working **at the moment**,' she said.	She said he was working **at that moment**.
here	there
'The children are **here**,' he said.	He said the children were **there**.

Unit 17

> **Reported Speech: Questions**
>
> When we report questions, changes in tenses, pronouns, possessive adjectives, time and place are the same as in reported statements. In reported questions, the verb follows the subject as in ordinary statements and we do not use question marks.
>
> When a direct question has a question word, we use this word in the reported question.
> '**When** did you decide to study Spanish?' he asked.
> He asked **when** I had decided to study Spanish.
>
> When a direct question does not have a question word, we use *if* or *whether* in the reported question.
> '*Is your sister at home?*' he asked.
> He asked **if/whether** my sister was at home.

Grammar Exercises

2 Circle the correct words.

1. You didn't **say / tell** me you were ill.
2. My dad **said / told** there was a message for me.
3. She **says / tells** too many silly stories.
4. Ben **said / told** Monica that he liked her.
5. Who **said / told** you could do that?
6. Why didn't you **say / tell** you were hungry?
7. I didn't **say / tell** anyone I was going on holiday.
8. Our teacher **said / told** us we had lots of homework.
9. Did anyone **say / tell** you about the project?
10. My sister **said / told** that she wasn't having a birthday party.

3 Complete the dialogues using reported speech and the words in brackets.

1. **A:** Susan has two brothers.
   B: But you said 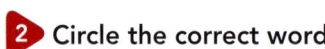 _she had three_____. (three)
2. **A:** We're going to Aunt Hilda's house.
   B: But you said _____. (Grandma's house)
3. **A:** Thomas has bought a new skateboard.
   B: But you said _____. (a bike)
4. **A:** The kids have been sleeping.
   B: But they said _____. (play)
5. **A:** I broke my mobile phone.
   B: But you said _____. (laptop)
6. **A:** We were watching TV.
   B: But your mum said _____. (playing games)
7. **A:** Dan can only speak Italian and French.
   B: But he said _____. (Chinese)
8. **A:** We'll go to the beach tomorrow.
   B: But you said _____. (today)

4 Complete the sentences. Make the correct changes in time and place.

1. 'I don't like it here,' he said.
   He said he didn't like it _____.
2. 'We're going home today,' they said.
   They said they were going home _____.
3. 'I felt ill last night,' she said.
   She said she had felt ill _____.
4. 'I'll buy you a present tomorrow,' he told her.
   He told her he'd buy her a present _____.
5. 'This is great,' she said.
   She said _____ was great.
6. 'I told Tom about it two weeks ago,' he said.
   He said he had told Tom about it _____.
7. 'I'm working at the moment,' she said.
   She said she was working _____.
8. 'Your bag is here on the chair,' he said to me.
   He told me my bag was _____ on the chair.

5 Rewrite the sentences in reported speech.

1. 'I was really happy there,' he said.
   He said _____.
2. 'We love this place,' they said.
   They said _____.
3. 'I went to France last month,' she said.
   She said _____.
4. 'He'll have a party next week,' I said.
   I said _____.
5. 'She's sleeping at the moment,' he said.
   He said _____.
6. 'We are going out tonight,' they said.
   They said _____.
7. 'Yesterday was a beautiful day,' she said.
   She said _____.
8. 'I can't help you now,' he said to me.
   He said _____.

6 Complete the reported questions so that they mean the same as the direct questions.

1. 'What time did you get up this morning?' she asked me.
   She asked me _____.
2. 'Do you have any money?' he asked her.
   He asked her _____.
3. 'What do you think about this film?' I asked him.
   I asked him _____.
4. 'Where is my computer?' she asked me.
   She asked me _____.
5. 'When are you leaving?' he asked me.
   He asked me _____.
6. 'What are you going to do?' she asked him.
   She asked him _____.
7. 'Are you having fun?' he asked her.
   He asked her _____.
8. 'Did you enjoy the show?' she asked me.
   She asked me _____.

Unit 17

7 Change the dialogue into reported speech.

1. **Mark:** 'How old are you?'
   He asked her _how old she was_.
2. **Sue:** 'I'm seventeen.'
   She said _____.
3. **Mark:** 'Can you sing?'
   He asked her _____.
4. **Sue:** 'I can sing very well.'
   She said _____.
5. **Mark:** 'What is your favourite kind of music?'
   He asked her _____.
6. **Sue:** 'I like hip-hop and jazz.'
   She said _____.
7. **Mark:** 'Do you want to join my band?'
   He asked her _____.
8. **Sue:** 'No, I don't want to.'
   She said _____.

Vocabulary

Collocations & Expressions

8 Match to form phrases.

1. to work   a a product
2. to lay   b your notice
3. to launch   c the sack
4. to reject   d an offer
5. to be in   e staff
6. to take on   f off
7. to get   g shifts
8. to hand in   h charge

9 Complete the sentences with the correct form of the phrases from 8.

1. When you _____, you work either during the day or night.
2. If you _____, that means you formally leave your job.
3. The person who is _____ is the boss.
4. When a company _____, they make it available to the public.
5. If you _____, you decide that it isn't important enough for you to accept.
6. When somebody _____, they are told to leave their job.
7. When a company _____ some workers, it stops employing them.
8. When a company _____, it employs new workers.

Exam Practice

10 Complete the second sentence so that it has a similar meaning to the first sentence, using the word given. Do not change the word given. You must use between two and five words.

1 'Have you done your homework?' my dad asked me.
   had
   My dad asked me _____ my homework.

2 'We're going skiing next month,' she said.
   following
   She said they _____ month.

3 'We have to go soon,' said John.
   they
   John said _____ soon.

4 'She may be lost,' I said.
   might
   I said that _____ lost.

5 'What time did you get home?' she asked me.
   had
   She asked me _____ got home.

6 'The boys are expecting a party tonight,' he said.
   were
   He said that _____ a party that night.

7 'Your book is here on the sofa,' she said to me.
   there
   She said that _____ on the sofa.

8 'Does she have any experience?' he asked me.
   whether
   He asked me _____ any experience.

11 Use the word in capitals to form a word that fits in the gap.

1 You need a _____ of skills to work here. **COMBINE**
2 I'm working on an _____ about working teenagers. **ASSIGN**
3 _____, the more you work, the more you get paid. **BASIC**
4 Unfortunately, your application was _____. **SUCCESS**
5 Tony's _____ led him to apply for the museum job. **CURIOUS**
6 I don't believe that – it's an _____ story! **CREDIBLE**
7 That was an _____ meal. Well done! **EXCEL**
8 Terry is really _____ about art. **PASSION**

Writing

12 Write six reported speech sentences in your notebook which are true for you. Here are some ideas:
- What was the first thing somebody said to you today/yesterday?
- What was the first thing you said today/yesterday?
- What questions were you asked yesterday?
- What questions did you ask?

Unit 18

Awareness

1 Which of these sentences are correct (C) and incorrect (I)?

1. I asked her help me. ___
2. She told him sitting down. ___
3. Did I remind you to call your mother? ___
4. You promised to take me out. ___
5. Why did he insist on stay so long? ___
6. I suggested going to bed early that night. ___
7. He asked me to not shout. ___
8. They refused leaving at the end of the show. ___
9. Did he accuse you of lying? ___
10. The police officer told us to go home. ___

How many did you get right? ☐

Grammar

Reported Speech: Commands & Requests

When we report commands, we usually use *tell* + object + full infinitive.
'Be quiet!' he shouted at me.
He **told me to be quiet**.
'Don't forget to post the letter,' he said to his sister.
He **told his sister not to forget** to post the letter.

When we report a request, we usually use *ask* + object + full infinitive.
'Can you help me do my homework, please?' she asked.
She **asked me to help** her do her homework.
(Also: She **asked if I could help** her do her homework.)
'Please don't go to work,' she said.
She **asked me not to go** to work.

Reported Speech: Reporting Verbs

Apart from the verbs *say*, *tell* and *ask*, we can also use other verbs to report what someone says more accurately. Notice the different structures.

verb + full infinitive	
decide	'I think I'll buy a new car,' he said. He **decided to buy** a new car.
refuse	'I won't buy a new car,' he said. He **refused to buy** a new car.
offer	'Shall I fix it?' he said. He **offered to fix** it.
promise	'Don't worry, I'll buy a new car,' he said. He **promised to buy** a new car.
verb + object + full infinitive	
advise	'If I were you, I'd buy a new car,' he said. He **advised me to buy** a new car.
remind	'Don't forget to buy a new car,' he said. He **reminded me to buy** a new car.

verb + gerund (-ing)	
deny	'I didn't crash the car,' he said. He **denied crashing** the car.
suggest	'Let's buy a new car,' he said. He **suggested buying** a new car.
verb + preposition + gerund (-ing)	
apologise for	'I'm sorry I crashed your car,' he said. He **apologised for crashing** my car.
insist on	'Don't be silly. I will buy a new car for you,' he said. He **insisted on buying** a new car for me.
verb + object + preposition + gerund (-ing)	
accuse sb of	'I'm sure you crashed my car,' he said. He **accused me of crashing** his car.
congratulate sb on	'You bought a new car. Well done!' he said. He **congratulated me on buying** a new car.

Grammar Exercises

2 Circle the correct words.

1 Simon refused **to help / helping** me.
2 You **promised / suggested** to buy me a new hat.
3 Never apologise for **tell / telling** the truth.
4 My doctor **insisted / advised** me to eat less bread.
5 The head teacher congratulated Tom on **pass / passing** his exams.
6 Gary **denied / refused** stealing my calculator.
7 I accused her of **be / being** rude.
8 Sara didn't remind me **phone / to phone** her yesterday.
9 She **offered / advised** to pay for my ticket.
10 We decided **going / to go** to the art exhibition.

3 Complete the sentences with the correct form of the verbs in brackets.

1 My dad congratulated me on _____ (win) the race.
2 Why did he decide _____ (move) to Italy?
3 Karen advised her brother _____ (work) on his English verbs.
4 The children denied _____ (break) the plate.
5 She apologised for _____ (call) so early in the morning.
6 I was accused of _____ (cheat) in the exam.
7 Dan offered _____ (carry) Stella's bag home for her.
8 Did you remind him _____ (take) his sports kit to school?
9 I suggested _____ (go) to the beach, but nobody was interested.
10 They refused _____ (stand) up until the lights were on.

Unit 18

4 Change the sentences from direct speech to reported speech. Use these verbs.

> accuse   advise   apologise   congratulate   deny   refuse   remind   suggest

1 'You ate the last sandwich,' she said to me.
She _____.

2 'Don't forget to bring some fresh water,' he said to her.
He _____.

3 'You shouldn't drink so much coffee,' the doctor told me.
The doctor _____.

4 'I'm really sorry that I got angry,' I said to her.
I _____.

5 'I didn't burn the cakes,' she said.
She _____.

6 'Why don't we go shopping?' he said.
He _____.

7 'You finished the project. Well done!' she said to him.
She _____.

8 'No, I won't come with you to the cinema,' he said to me.
He _____.

5 Rewrite the commands and requests in reported speech.

1 'Don't touch that button!' she said to him.
_____

2 'Finish your dinner,' he said to me.
_____

3 'Please don't do that,' he said to her.
_____

4 'Don't forget to close the window,' she said to him.
_____

5 'Work harder,' he said to her.
_____

6 'Please be careful,' she said to me.
_____

6 Find the mistakes and correct the sentences.

1 He refused talking about his experiences.
_____

2 She asked me work a little longer.
_____

3 They advised me taking an umbrella.
_____

4 You promised give me your old skateboard.
_____

5 He told his mother to not wake him up early.
_____

6 Did you remember Sonia to speak to her teacher?
_____

7 Change the reported speech into direct speech.

1. Carla asked Ben what they should do. Ben suggested going to the park.
   Carla: What should we do?
   Ben: Let's go to the park.
2. Sam accused Mark of stealing his book. Mark denied it.
   Sam: _____
   Mark: _____
3. Dave asked Maria if she wanted to go out or stay in. She decided to stay in.
   Dave: _____
   Maria: _____
4. The teacher told Dan to go home. But Dan refused.
   Teacher: _____
   Dan: _____
5. Fred apologised for forgetting to buy a newspaper. Tina reminded him the shop was open until 10 pm.
   Fred: _____
   Tina: _____
6. Harry offered to buy Karen a sandwich. Karen insisted on buying her own.
   Harry: _____
   Karen: _____
7. Grandma congratulated me on passing all my exams, and promised to buy me a present.
   Grandma: _____
   _____
8. Ben asked when they were going to the beach. Dad promised to take them the next day.
   Ben: _____
   Dad: _____

Vocabulary

Prepositions

8 Complete the phrases with these prepositions. You will need to use some prepositions more than once.

| in | of | on | to |

1. find a solution _____
2. _____ my opinion
3. to be out _____ work
4. to be _____ debt
5. to react _____ something
6. _____ behalf of
7. reach the top _____
8. arrive/be _____ time

9 Complete the sentences with the correct form of the phrases from 8.

1. If you don't arrive at work _____, you won't have a job for long.
2. It took a long time to _____ the problem, but we did it.
3. How did Simon _____ that difficult situation? Did he panic?
4. At the age of 50, Julia had finally _____ her chosen career.
5. _____, that was a really stupid decision.
6. If you have good skills, you won't _____ for very long.
7. _____ everyone here, I'd like to thank you for all your hard work.
8. Don't use credit cards if you don't want to _____.

Unit 18

Exam Practice

10 Complete the second sentence so that it has a similar meaning to the first sentence, using the word given. Do not change the word given. You must use between two and five words.

1 'I'm sorry I'm late,' she said.
   apologised
   She _____ late.

2 'No, I won't do what you say,' she said to him.
   refused
   She _____ said.

3 'Let's play a game,' said John.
   playing
   John _____ a game.

4 'You should go and see a doctor,' I said to her.
   her
   I _____ and see a doctor.

5 'I didn't make a mistake,' she said.
   making
   She _____ a mistake.

6 'Shall I make a cup of coffee?' he said.
   offered
   He _____ a cup of coffee.

7 I hope you can solve my problem.
   find
   I hope you can _____ my problem.

8 At the moment, Greg hasn't got a job.
   out
   Greg is _____ at the moment.

11 Complete the sentences with the word that best fits each gap.

1 I'd like to thank you _____ behalf of everyone here.
2 She reminded me _____ take a shower before I went out.
3 It's the most interesting job in the world, _____ my opinion.
4 It took five days to reach the top _____ the mountain.
5 Congratulations _____ your recent success.
6 I apologised _____ missing the start of the meeting.
7 My boss asked me _____ I could work on Sunday.
8 'Don't forget to send that email,' she _____ to her secretary.

Writing

12 Write six sentences in your notebook which are true for you. Report what was said the last time someone

- apologised to you.
- promised something to you.
- gave you some advice.
- made a suggestion to you.
- accused you of something.
- congratulated you.

Unit 19

Awareness

1 Which of these sentences are correct (C) and incorrect (I)?

1. If you will travel first class, you will be more comfortable. ___
2. They won't let you in if you don't have a ticket. ___
3. We'd stay in a hotel if it hadn't cost so much money. ___
4. I wouldn't have known if she hadn't told me. ___
5. If you heat ice, it melts. ___
6. She'd come if you would ask her. ___
7. If you would have had lunch, you wouldn't be hungry now. ___
8. If I was you, I wouldn't do that. ___
9. Don't let him in the house if he calls round. ___
10. We'll show you the city if you would visit. ___

How many did you get right? ☐

Grammar

Zero Conditional

If clause	Main clause
present simple	present simple

We use the zero conditional to talk about an action or situation that is always true. We can use *when* instead of *if*.
If you **ride** a bike, you **don't pollute** the atmosphere.
When you **ride** a bike, you **don't pollute** the atmosphere.

First Conditional

If clause	Main clause
present tense	*will* + bare infinitive

We use the first conditional to talk about an action or situation that will probably happen now or in the future.
*If it **rains**, the washing **will get** wet.*
*If the weather **isn't good**, we **won't go** out.*

We can use *can, could, may* or *might* in the main clause instead of *will*. We can also use an imperative.
*If you want to help your mum, you **could** wash some vegetables.*
*If you don't want to come with us, **stay** here.*

Second Conditional

If clause	Main clause
past tense	*would* + bare infinitive

We use the second conditional to talk about an action or a situation
• that probably won't happen now or in the future.
*You **would make** more money if you **worked** more hours.*
• that is impossible or imaginary in the present or in the future.
*If I **owned** a yacht, I'**d sail** around the world.*

We can also use the second conditional to give advice.
*If I **were** you, I'**d eat** more fruit.*

We can use *could* or *might* in the main clause instead of *would*.
*You **could visit** your cousins if you **went** to Australia.*
*I **might go** to university if I **passed** my final exams.*

> **Note**
> We usually use *were* for all persons in second conditional sentences.
> *If Jim **were** older, he'**d be able to** play this game.*

Unit 19

Third Conditional

If clause	Main clause
past perfect tense	would + have + past participle

We use the third conditional to talk about events or situations in the past that could have happened but didn't.
These are always hypothetical things because we cannot change the past.
If my dad **had not met** my mum, I **would not have been** born. (I was born because my dad met my mum.)

We can use *could* or *might* in the main clause instead of *would*.
We **could have bought** that house if we **had had** more money.
If the film **had been shown** earlier, I **might have seen** it.

Mixed Conditionals

If clause	Main clause
past perfect tense	would + bare infinitive

A mixed conditional is where the two clauses in a conditional sentence refer to different times.
We use a mixed conditional to express the present result of a hypothetical past event or situation.
If I **hadn't stolen** that bike, I **wouldn't be** in the police station now.

Grammar Exercises

2 Circle the correct words.

1. When you arrive, they **check / would check** your passport.
2. I **would be / am** very angry if you broke my laptop.
3. If I **have / had** a dog, I'd call it Samantha.
4. You **would be / will be** fine if you don't panic.
5. If she **ate / is eating** less, she would be healthier.
6. I would have come with you if you **had bought / buy** me a ticket.
7. If you **arrive / arrived** late, you have to wait until the interval.
8. Try climbing if you **want / wanted** an exciting hobby.
9. If they hadn't missed that plane, they **would be / will be** in Italy now.
10. We could have won if we **had worked / work** together as a team.

3 Complete the sentences using the First Conditional.

1. She _____ (like) it if you _____ (give) her flowers.
2. If you _____ (not stop) shouting, you _____ (hurt) your throat.
3. We _____ (not get) a seat at the show if we _____ (not leave) now.
4. I _____ (write) your essay for you if you _____ (feel) ill.
5. They _____ (be) angry if you _____ (not tell) them about the accident.
6. If you _____ (not know) what something is, you _____ (find) the information on the Internet.
7. If they _____ (like) your story, they _____ (publish) it.
8. He _____ (not go) to the match if it _____ (be) still raining.

4 Complete the second sentences using the Second Conditional.

1 He trains very hard; that's why he is so fit.
   If he _____ so hard, he _____ so fit.
2 She doesn't have to work, so she spends a lot of time with her friends.
   She _____ so much time with her friends if she _____ work.
3 They play well together; that's why they are champions.
   If they _____ well together, they _____ champions.
4 We go to bed early, so we get up easily the next day.
   We _____ easily the next day if we _____ to bed early.
5 I can't drink this coffee because it's too hot.
   If this coffee _____ so hot, I _____ drink it.
6 His computer isn't working, so he can't read his emails.
   He _____ his emails if his computer _____ working.
7 They have parties every night, so they are tired every day.
   If they _____ parties every night, they _____ tired every day.
8 He doesn't own a car, so he doesn't drive to work.
   He _____ to work if he _____ a car.

5 Complete the sentences using the Third Conditional.

1 If we _____ (not buy) tickets, we _____ (not be) allowed inside.
2 We _____ (bring) some food if we _____ (know) you didn't have any.
3 If I _____ (hear) that you were in hospital, I _____ (visit) you.
4 You _____ (not be) disappointed if you _____ (come) to the exhibition with us.
5 If we _____ (have) any more luggage, we _____ (have to) pay extra.
6 She _____ (not make) so much cake if you _____ (tell) her you didn't want a party.
7 If we _____ (know) it would make us ill, we _____ (not eat) it.
8 I _____ (help) you if you _____ (ask) me.

6 Complete the sentences with the correct form of the verbs in brackets.

1 If you _____ (not drink) so much coffee, you would be feeling fine now.
2 I'd be rich now if I _____ (buy) this house years ago.
3 If Mario _____ (go) to university, he'd have a good job now.
4 She _____ (not be) in hospital now if she had been wearing a helmet.
5 If you had seen the film, you _____ (know) what we are talking about.
6 We'd be lying on the beach now if we _____ (not miss) the plane.
7 Dan would be playing professional golf now if he _____ (start) learning when he was a boy.
8 If I had told her about the meeting, she _____ (be) here today.

Unit 19 111

Unit 19

7 Find the mistakes and correct the sentences.

1 If you will want to play, you will need some training shoes.

2 The tickets would have been cheaper if you had book them online.

3 If I was you, I would speak to her about it.

4 We will be there now if we hadn't set off late.

5 You can pick up a leaflet when you'll be there.

6 If I had had more money, I'll buy a leather jacket.

7 Mum might have let us go out if the weather was being better.

8 If I had studied harder at school, I'll be a millionaire now.

Vocabulary

Word formation

8 Match the words with their meanings.

1 accommodate
2 agent
3 architect
4 board
5 depart
6 land
7 mountain
8 tour

a to travel around
b to provide with a place to stay
c to return to the ground after flying
d a person or company who does something on your behalf
e to get on a plane, boat, or train
f a person who designs buildings
g a very high hill
h to leave

9 Use the word in capitals to form a word that fits in the gap.

1 The _____ in Barcelona is amazing. **ARCHITECT**
2 The flight was very smooth and enjoyable, but the _____ was rough. **LAND**
3 We need to find some _____ before it gets too late. **ACCOMMODATE**
4 My aunt works for a big travel _____ in London. **AGENT**
5 The west of Scotland is a very _____ area. **MOUNTAIN**
6 Have you got our _____ passes? We should hurry. **BOARD**
7 I hope our _____ is not delayed again. **DEPART**
8 There are a lot of _____ visiting London at this time of year. **TOUR**

Exam Practice

10 Complete the second sentence so that it has a similar meaning to the first sentence, using the word given. Do not change the word given. You must use between two and five words.

1. You failed the test because you didn't study.
   had
   If _____, you wouldn't have failed the test.

2. My advice to you is – don't do it.
   were
   If _____, I wouldn't do it.

3. I didn't see her, so I didn't give her the message.
   seen
   If _____, I would have given her the message.

4. Tom can't drive, so he has to ride his bike everywhere.
   have
   If Tom could drive, _____ ride his bike everywhere.

5. Wearing a helmet will reduce the chance of injury.
   if
   You will reduce the chance of injury _____ a helmet.

6. My phone isn't working, so I can't call you.
   could
   If my phone was working, _____ you.

7. Dad didn't go to the bank, so he didn't have any cash.
   would
   Dad _____ if he had gone to the bank.

8. She won't eat that because it has meat in it.
   have
   She would eat that _____ meat in it.

11 Choose the correct answers.

1. If you recycle, you ___ protect the planet.
   a helping   b help   c helps   d helped

2. He ___ fall if he is not careful.
   a will   b would   c is   d has

3. If she ___ the solution, she would tell you.
   a knows   b known   c knew   d know

4. We could have stayed longer if we had ___ time.
   a have   b having   c has   d had

5. If the town hadn't been destroyed, it would ___ be beautiful.
   a now   b still   c yet   d even

6. I ___ give money to the poor if I had enough of it.
   a would   b will   c have   d had

7. You could ___ won if you had run faster.
   a may   b have   c had   d easily

8. I wouldn't tell him if I ___ you.
   a am   b was   c be   d were

Writing

12 Complete these sentences in your notebook so that they are true for you.

1. If I had a billion euros, ___.
2. I would be very angry if ___.
3. If it is sunny this weekend, ___.
4. If I could live anywhere in the world, ___.
5. If I had been born 500 years ago, ___.
6. I'll laugh if ___.

Unit 20

Awareness

1 Which of these sentences are correct (C) and incorrect (I)?

1. If you hadn't eaten so much, you'll feel better now. ___
2. Provided everyone is ready, we'll leave at 5 pm. ___
3. Supposing you could go anywhere, where would you go? ___
4. I wish you don't tell me that news. ___
5. He's happy to help, provided you paid him. ___
6. If only she tried harder, she'd do well. ___
7. Don't touch that, otherwise you might broke it. ___
8. I'll buy it as long as it isn't too expensive. ___
9. They won't be able to come otherwise they're too busy. ___
10. He wishes he has longer arms. ___

How many did you get right? ☐

Grammar

Conditionals without If

We can use *provided/providing that* and *as long as* to replace *if* in first conditional sentences.
Provided I have enough cash, I'll buy you lunch.
Providing that you promise to be quiet, we'll go to the library this afternoon.
As long as we get there on time, we won't miss the start of the film.

We can use *unless* in first and second conditional sentences. It means the same as *if not*.
She won't sleep well **unless** she does some exercise.
Unless you have asked for permission, you won't be allowed into the building.

We can use *otherwise* to replace an *if* clause. It means *if not*.
If you don't take your binoculars, you won't be able to see the players.
Take your binoculars. **Otherwise**, you won't be able to see the players.

We can use *supposing* in all conditional sentences. The main clause is usually a question. It means *imagine* or *what if*.
Supposing the package doesn't arrive, what will we do?
Supposing you hadn't seen the warning sign, what would have happened?
Supposing you were lost in a strange city, who would you call?

Wish & If only

We use *wish* to talk about a situation or an action we aren't happy about, or to say how we would like something to be different.

We use *wish* + a past tense when we talk about the present or the future.
I **wish** I **knew** how to speak Chinese.

We use *wish* + a past perfect tense when we talk about the past.
I **wish** I **hadn't eaten** so much last night.

We use *wish* + *would* + bare infinitive when we talk about other people's annoying habits or to say that we would like something to be different in the future. We use it for actions, not states. We can only use *wish* + *would* when the subjects are different.
I **wish** they **wouldn't let** dogs into parks.
I **wish** the weather **would get** better.

We can use *if only* instead of *wish* in affirmative and negative sentences.
If only I had a fast car.
If only I was taller.

Grammar Exercises

2 Circle the correct words.

1 You had better eat your dinner **provided / unless / otherwise** you can't have any dessert.
2 He won't go to the party **provided / unless / as long as** you go with him.
3 I'll tidy your room **as long as / unless / supposing** you help me with my project.
4 **Providing / Supposing / Unless** it snows tomorrow, what should we do?
5 **Provided that / Supposing / Unless** you change your clothes, you can go out.
6 She won't be happy **provided / otherwise / unless** we go to the museum.
7 We'll go to the beach tomorrow **providing / supposing / unless** the weather is good enough.
8 **As long as / Supposing / Providing** the campsite had been closed, where would you have gone?

3 Complete the second sentence so that it has a similar meaning to the first sentence.

1 If you are not ready, we won't leave.
Unless _____.
2 He won't sell his bike if you don't offer him more money.
Unless _____.
3 If she doesn't have an umbrella, she'll get wet.
Unless _____.
4 We won't go to school if it doesn't stop snowing.
Unless _____.
5 If you don't get that car fixed, you might have an accident.
Unless _____.
6 They won't come if you don't send them an invitation.
Unless _____.
7 If he hasn't got the time, he won't do the job.
Unless _____.
8 I won't go on holiday if I don't feel better.
Unless _____.

4 Match to form sentences. They are joined with **as long as**.

1 You can play your music
2 I'll lend you £5
3 We can play football
4 They'll give me the job
5 He can borrow my bike
6 I'll cook dinner
7 She doesn't have to finish it today
8 They won't be hungry at lunch time

a he rides carefully.
b I work on Sundays.
c it doesn't rain.
d they have a big breakfast.
e you pay me back tomorrow.
f you play it quietly.
g she finishes it tomorrow.
h you do the washing up.

5 Circle the correct words.

1 I wish I **can / could** run faster.
2 I wish Simon **doesn't speak / didn't speak** so quickly.
3 She wishes she **learnt / had learnt** how to drive.
4 If only I could **join / joined** you on your trip.
5 He really wishes he **didn't forget / hadn't forgotten** his wallet.
6 If only Mark **bought / had bought** that house two years ago.
7 I wish you **didn't say / hadn't said** anything to her.
8 If only summer **can / could** last a little bit longer.

Unit 20 115

Unit 20

6 Complete the sentences with the correct form of the verbs in brackets.
1. I wish I _____ (can) swim with dolphins.
2. My mum wishes she _____ (study) harder at school.
3. James wishes he _____ (not shout) at his sister – now he feels bad.
4. If only I _____ (have) more time to finish this project.
5. I wish my parents _____ (give) me more pocket money.
6. If only we _____ (not lose) our passports.
7. I wish the people across the street _____ (stop) arguing.
8. My brother wishes he _____ (be) as fast a runner as me.

7 Complete the sentences with the word that best fits each gap.
1. I _____ I could speak Portuguese.
2. He wouldn't do it _____ he really wanted to.
3. Provided _____ you study hard, you'll pass without any problem.
4. Supposing you won the lottery, what _____ you do with the money?
5. If _____ I had known about this years ago.
6. You had better go to bed now, _____ you'll be exhausted in the morning.
7. She'll agree to help you _____ that you ask her politely.
8. You can use my towel _____ long as you wash it afterwards.

Vocabulary

Phrasal verbs

8 Complete the phrasal verbs with these verbs. You will need to use some of them more than once.

check   drop   get   put   see   set

1. _____ around – to move from place to place
2. _____ off – to take someone somewhere and leave them
3. _____ in – to arrive at a hotel
4. _____ on – to board a plane, train
5. _____ out – to begin a journey
6. _____ off – to wave goodbye to someone leaving from an airport, station
7. _____ up – to assemble or build something
8. _____ away – to escape

9 Complete the sentences with the correct form of the phrasal verbs from 8.
1. It's an old car, but it works fine for _____ me _____ town.
2. They _____ a new skyscraper next to the airport.
3. We _____ to the hotel just after midnight.
4. I won't come and _____ you _____ at the station tomorrow because I hate saying goodbye.
5. The taxi _____ us _____ in the centre of the city.
6. It will soon be time for us to _____ the plane.
7. I like to _____ from the big city every summer, and relax on a quiet island.
8. If we _____ at around 5 am, we'll get there before noon.

Exam Practice

10 Complete the second sentence so that it has a similar meaning to the first sentence, using the word given. Do not change the word given. You must use between two and five words.

1. Darren forgot his football boots and he regrets it.
   forgotten
   Darren wishes _____ his football boots.

2. I wish I could ride a motorbike.
   only
   If _____ ride a motorbike.

3. I am sorry that you didn't tell me.
   told
   I wish _____ me.

4. She regrets not going to the show.
   wishes
   She _____ to the show.

5. It is a pity that you forgot to phone me.
   remembered
   If only _____ to phone me.

6. If you don't frighten the dog, it won't bite you.
   long
   The dog won't bite you _____ don't frighten it.

7. They won't let you in if you are not wearing smart clothes.
   unless
   They won't let you in _____ smart clothes.

8. If I have time, I'll go and visit Grandma.
   that
   I'll go and visit Grandma _____ I have time.

11 Use the word in capitals to form a word that fits in the gap.

1. The _____ of earth is increasing every year. **POPULATE**
2. That is a very _____ dress. **COLOUR**
3. The most _____ thing about him is his intelligence. **IMPRESS**
4. The water in this village is heated _____. **NATURE**
5. We haven't got the necessary _____ to finish this job. **EQUIP**
6. The temperature dropped _____ when the sun went down. **DRAMATIC**
7. We relaxed and enjoyed the _____ out of the train window. **SCENE**
8. How many _____ are staying in this hotel at the moment? **TRAVEL**

Writing

12 Write three things in your notebook that you wish you had/hadn't done in the past, and three things that you wish were different about the present.

I wish I had gone to bed earlier last night.
I wish I wasn't so tired.

Unit 20 117

Review 5

Grammar

1 Rewrite the sentences in reported speech.

1 'You can go to the cinema tomorrow,' she said to me.
  She told me that _____.
2 'We were feeling very relaxed,' they said.
  They said that _____.
3 'Do you have any sisters?' he asked me.
  He asked me _____.
4 'They are leaving next month,' he said.
  He said that _____.
5 'Last week we went to a great party,' she said.
  She said that _____.
6 'What were you doing last night?' he asked me.
  He asked me _____.
7 'I have never seen this before,' she said.
  She said that _____.
8 'Did you enjoy your meal?' she asked them.
  She asked them _____.

2 Complete the sentences with the correct form of the verbs in brackets.

1 The police accused Mario of _____ (steal) a sandwich.
2 I told you _____ (not open) that window!
3 She congratulated her friend on _____ (pass) all her exams.
4 He offered _____ (give) me a lift home in his car.
5 Why did you suggest _____ (come) here? It's boring!
6 My mum asked me _____ (clean) the kitchen.
7 Greg denied _____ (tell) my secret to everyone.
8 The teacher advised me _____ (take) extra Spanish lessons.

3 Match to form sentences.

1 If we are late,
2 When you press this button,
3 You wouldn't have enjoyed it
4 If they were more adventurous,
5 If I were you,
6 She'd sing us a song
7 If you had finished your lunch,
8 If I had known you were coming,

a I would apologise immediately.
b they would enjoy exploring new places.
c if she had her guitar with her.
d if you had gone on your own.
e the door opens.
f I'd have baked a cake.
g you wouldn't be hungry now.
h we'll have to catch the next train.

4 Circle the correct words.

1 She **said / told** that she liked chocolate cake.
2 They insisted on **stay / staying** until the end.
3 We'll do it **provided / supposing** you agree.
4 **If only / Otherwise** she took her studies more seriously.
5 You'll feel better if you **take / will take** a walk in the park.
6 She asked me when I **decide / had decided** to join the club.
7 I wish **was / would** be older.

5 Look at the situations and complete the sentences using the word in bold.

1. I really regret not joining the swimming club.
   only
   If _____ the swimming club.

2. Dan forgot his wallet, so he can't buy anything.
   forgotten
   Dan wishes _____.

3. We can't hear what the new teacher is saying.
   speak
   We wish _____ more loudly.

4. She is upset because she lost her passport.
   only
   If _____.

5. Our neighbours are making a lot of noise.
   wouldn't
   I wish _____ so much noise.

6. He wants to drive a car, but he doesn't know how.
   knew
   He wishes _____.

7. It's been raining for days, and it makes me unhappy.
   would
   If only _____.

8. I can't dance.
   could
   I wish _____.

6 Find the mistakes and correct the sentences.

1. Supposing you broke your dad's computer, what did you do?

2. You can swim in our pool if you'll come and visit us.

3. He told he had been shopping in town.

4. I suggest to go to the cinema.

5. What did that man say you?

6. I didn't buy that bike if I were you.

7. She wishes she has a red sports car.

8. You didn't remind me buying some milk.

Review 5

Exam Practice

7 For questions 1–10, read the text below. Use the word given in capitals at the end of each line to form a word that fits in the gap in the same line. There is an example at the beginning (0).

No gain without pain

In these days of (0) ___economic___ hardship it is very difficult for charities to   ECONOMY
raise money. 'Charity fatigue' means ordinary appeals have become increasingly
(1) _____, and new ways of raising money have to be dreamt up.   EFFECT
(2) _____ newspapers, which employ many creative people, are playing an   NATION
an important role in developing these new ideas. For example, newspapers regularly organise
unusual or demanding expeditions for their journalists and other celebrities to take part in.
The hope is that (3) _____ newspaper readers will make large   WEALTH
(4) _____ to the cause – and they frequently do!   DONATE
On one such expedition, a group of journalists, acting as a well-known newspaper's
(5) _____, climbed Mount Everest. Detailed reports of how   REPRESENT
(6) _____ became more difficult during the climb appeared daily in the   BREATH
newspaper, together with (7) _____ accounts of how each member of   PERSON
the team was coping. As can be imagined, those participating went through a great deal
of physical and (8) _____ suffering. And the readers were hooked!   PSYCHOLOGY
As the climb progressed, readers found the (9) _____ to donate money.   INSPIRE
It appeared that they felt a greater (10) _____ to give money to the   OBLIGE
appeal as the climbers' suffering increased.

8 For questions 11–22, read the text below and decide which answer (A, B, C or D) best fits each gap. There is an example at the beginning (0).

Flora and fauna at risk

(0) __ many leading zoologists and botanists have expressed their concern about the (11) __ of endangered species, most of the measures taken to (12) __ these species against extinction have had little effect.

From the (13) __ of the sea to mountain slopes, tens of thousands of species have become extinct in the (14) __ 300 years. Thousands have died out even before they have been (15) __. Many experts now believe that mankind has reached the (16) __ of no return.

The greatest threat to plants and animals is the destruction of the planet's rainforests. On (17) __, an area of forest the size of Switzerland is destroyed every two and a half years. (18) __ regions are cleared every month, which means that animals have nothing to eat and birds have nowhere to (19) __.

Now CITES (Convention on International Trade in Endangered Species) has (20) __ on the responsibility of getting 800 species of animals and plants (21) __ from international trade. This is a step in the right direction, but should they fail, the (22) __ of the wolf may only be heard on CD in future.

0	A	Nevertheless	B	However	C	Despite	(D)	Although
11	A	maintenance	B	preservation	C	upkeep	D	support
12	A	maintain	B	shield	C	conserve	D	protect
13	A	bed	B	foot	C	base	D	bottom
14	A	earlier	B	former	C	past	D	previous
15	A	found out	B	discovered	C	determined	D	invented
16	A	site	B	location	C	spot	D	point
17	A	average	B	normal	C	standard	D	typical
18	A	Total	B	Full	C	Entire	D	Complete
19	A	fly	B	grow	C	nest	D	flock
20	A	seen	B	turned	C	worked	D	taken
21	A	avoided	B	banned	C	stopped	D	prevented
22	A	grunt	B	roar	C	squeak	D	howl

Grammar

9 For questions 1–10, choose the word or phrase that best completes the sentence or conversation.

1 The head teacher told me ___.
  A behave better
  B behaving better
  C to behaving better
  D to behave better

2 'Will you come out with me tonight?'
  'OK, ___ we don't come home too late.'
  A as long as
  B otherwise
  C supposing
  D unless

3 'Thanks for remembering to bring your notes.'
  'I wouldn't have remembered if you ___ me.'
  A didn't remind
  B weren't reminding
  C hadn't reminded
  D haven't reminded

4 I'm tired. I ___ to bed so late.
  A only hadn't gone
  B wish I hadn't gone
  C wouldn't have gone
  D didn't have gone

5 The interviewer asked me ___ music.
  A did I like
  B would I liked
  C if I liked
  D do I like

6 'What are you cooking tonight?'
  'Nothing. You promised ___ to a restaurant!'
  A to take us
  B to have taken us
  C taking us
  D you took us

7 If I were you, I ___ so near the stage.
  A didn't sit
  B haven't sat
  C 'm not sitting
  D wouldn't sit

8 ___ everyone is comfortable, I'll begin.
  A Supposing
  B Otherwise
  C Provided
  D Unless

9 Tonya said ___ to basketball matches.
  A she enjoyed going
  B she enjoys to go
  C she is enjoying to go
  D she is enjoying to go

10 Mum suggested ___ a holiday.
  A to take
  B taking
  C took
  D I had taken

Vocabulary

10 For questions 11–20, choose the word or phrase that best completes the sentence.

11 He got the ___ from his job because he was always late.
  A bag
  B shoe
  C sack
  D fire

12 I'm bored of working here, so I'm handing in my ___ next week.
  A notice
  B purse
  C sign
  D advice

13 They had to ___ off a lot of staff last year because of the economy.
  A put
  B get
  C move
  D lay

14 ___ behalf of everyone here, thank you.
  A In
  B On
  C By
  D At

15 In my ___, you made the right decision.
  A opinion
  B brain
  C idea
  D thoughts

16 You can't ___ the plane with all that hand luggage.
  A mount
  B ride
  C board
  D climb

17 We were looking for ___ near the centre of town.
  A accommodation
  B room
  C house
  D sleeping

18 I'll ___ you off at the station, if you like.
  A put
  B push
  C drop
  D carry

19 What time did you ___ in to your hotel?
  A make
  B check
  C sign
  D join

20 They are putting ___ a new building near our school.
  A out
  B on
  C over
  D up

Unit 21

Awareness

1 Which of these sentences are correct (C) and incorrect (I)?

1 We love the house next to the lake. ___
2 That's the man whose lawyer was a thief. ___
3 The police, that are still looking for the suspect, have no clues. ___
4 This is the place when the crime happened. ___
5 I'll never forget the day our flat was burgled. ___
6 My uncle, which is a judge, is a very clever man. ___
7 We interviewed a man looked very suspicious. ___
8 A pickpocket is a criminal who steals things from people's clothes. ___
9 I don't understand the reason why anyone would do that. ___
10 He made me watch a film which I didn't like it. ___

How many did you get right? ☐

Grammar
Relative Clauses

Relative clauses give more information about the subject or the object of a sentence. They are introduced by the following words:
- *who* for people
- *which* for things
- *whose* to show possession
- *when* for time
- *where* for places
- *why* for reason

Defining Relative Clauses

This type of relative clause gives us information that we need, to be able to understand who or what the speaker is talking about. We do not use commas to separate it from the rest of the sentence. We can use *that* instead of *who* and *which* in defining relative clauses.
That's the bank **where my dad works**.
We met some people **who/that were very strange**.

When *who*, *which* or *that* is the object of the relative clause, we can omit the relative pronoun.
He was the actor (**who**) they chose for the part.
The only kind of film (**which/that**) she doesn't like is horror.

Non-defining Relative Clauses

This type of relative clause gives us extra information which isn't necessary to be able to understand the meaning of the main clause. We use commas to separate it from the rest of the sentence.
My aunt, **who used to work in Brazil**, speaks perfect Portuguese.
His essay, **which is about prisons in the UK**, is very informative.

Grammar Exercises

2 Circle the correct words.

1 Is that the hotel **that / where** you met Greta?
2 The car, **which / who** was stolen last night, has already been found.
3 Do you remember the time **when / which** the school was closed at weekends?
4 Mr Smith, **who / that** was staying with us at the time, had a lot of money.
5 You never told me the reason **which / why** you left the computer club.
6 My stamp collection, **which / that** I keep in a box in a drawer, is quite valuable.
7 Evening is the time **when / where** I like to go for a walk in the park.
8 There's the man **where / that** I was telling you about.

3 Complete the sentences with the correct relative pronouns.

1 Arson is a crime _____ is very serious.
2 A detective is a police officer _____ solves crimes.
3 Is that the prison _____ your cousin is held?
4 The day _____ John went to court was very stressful.
5 That is the boy _____ mother is a lawyer.
6 Do you know the reason _____ they didn't arrest the suspect?
7 It was a difficult case, _____ involved a lot of police work.
8 I don't know anyone _____ has been a member of a jury.

4 Can we leave the pronouns out of these sentences? Write **Y** (yes) or **N** (no).

1 My mum, who makes amazing apple pie, has started her own business. ___
2 Can you remember the story that I told you? ___
3 I met a boy whose sister was in the Olympic basketball team. ___
4 The library where I usually study is closed today. ___
5 The reason why Tom isn't at school is because he is ill. ___
6 I'm thinking about that time when we all had a picnic by the river. ___
7 Did you see the man who stole your bag? ___
8 The car which was found in the playground was not damaged. ___

5 Match to form sentences. Complete the sentences with the correct pronouns.

1 A convict is a person
2 A prison is a place
3 A helmet is a hat
4 A burglar is a criminal
5 A judge is a person
6 Handcuffs are tools
7 A witness is a person
8 A court is a place

a _____ are used to tie suspect's hands together.
b _____ protects the head.
c _____ criminal trials happen.
d _____ saw a crime.
e _____ job it is to punish criminals.
f _____ prisoners are kept.
g _____ is in prison.
h _____ steals from houses.

6 Join the sentences using a relative pronoun. Remember to add commas if the clause is non-defining.

1 Simon is a great teacher. His wife is a judge.
   Simon, whose wife is a judge, is a great teacher.
2 Terry is the team captain. He is only eleven years old.

3 Lots of people break the law. They end up in prison.

4 Last winter was hard to forget. The weather was very cold.

5 Your computer has been found in the library. You have been looking for it.

6 They are building a factory on the park. I used to play there as a boy.

7 Mrs Smith is an athletics coach. Her son is in my class.

Unit 21

7 Find the mistakes and correct the sentences.

1 My old school, where I went there for six years, is being pulled down.

2 Lots of people which own cars don't really need them.

3 Do you know the reason why he handed in his notice for?

4 My best friend, dad is a policeman, was caught shoplifting.

5 He married a girl who she came from Argentina.

6 The CD player you gave me it doesn't work.

7 This skateboard, that I have had since I was seven, is my favourite object.

8 He really loves the car who he bought last month.

Vocabulary

Collocations & Expressions

8 Match to form expressions.

1 to accept   a the law
2 to be under   b (not) guilty
3 to have a police   c your ways
4 to break   d arrest
5 to let   e record
6 to plead   f a case
7 to solve   g somebody off
8 to mend   h responsibility for something

9 Complete the sentences with the correct form of the expressions from 8.

1 I hoped that the judge would put him in prison, but he _____ him _____.

2 You had better _____ your _____ or you will end up in prison one day.

3 Eventually, she _____ for the crime, and she was tried in court.

4 If you _____ to a crime, that means that you deny it.

5 Stevie had a _____ by the time he was 15.

6 Stop! You are _____ on suspicion of arson.

7 The detective was very happy when he finally _____.

8 Do not _____ – there is a good chance that you will be caught.

Exam Practice

10 Complete the second sentence so that it has a similar meaning to the first sentence, using the word given. Do not change the word given. You must use between two and five words.

1. Susan is the girl with the very fast motorbike.
   whose
   Susan is the girl _____ very fast.

2. We rented a villa in the mountains.
   that
   The villa _____ was in the mountains.

3. Tim is very brave and is an excellent police officer.
   who
   Tim, _____, is an excellent police officer.

4. He never buys stolen property.
   which
   He never _____ stolen.

5. She's sleeping in a caravan by the beach.
   where
   The caravan _____ is by the beach.

6. One of my dogs is a Chihuahua.
   which
   I have _____ a Chihuahua.

7. We went to Spain last year – it's our favourite country.
   went
   Spain, _____, is our favourite country.

8. They'll never forget winning the championship.
   won
   They'll never forget the time _____ the championship.

11 Complete the sentences with the word that best fits each gap.

1. An orphan is a child _____ parents are dead.
2. I have a friend _____ is very good at skiing.
3. There isn't much crime in the part of the city _____ I live.
4. Her favourite restaurant, _____ is quite expensive, is in London.
5. There's the dog _____ bit me last week.
6. Can you think of a reason _____ I shouldn't come with you?
7. That boy, _____ hair is dyed blue, is in trouble!
8. Did you enjoy the meal _____ I left out for you?

Writing

12 Write sentences in your notebook which are true for you. Use relative clauses.

- a day you will never forget *(when)*
- an activity you would like to try *(which/that)*
- a famous person you would like to meet *(who)*
- a place you would like to go *(where)*

Unit 22

Awareness

1 Which of these sentences are correct (C) and incorrect (I)?
1. She found her cat hiding under the bed. ___
2. The boy was given a medal felt very proud. ___
3. Not knowing what time the film started, we set off early. ___
4. The people employing last month were really good. ___
5. Not know what to do, I phoned my dad. ___
6. Seen from a distance, our house looks like a boat. ___
7. Watch the scene pass by the train window, I felt really happy. ___
8. The woman singing is my mother. ___
9. The boy chosen for the lead role is Samuel. ___
10. We weren't happy with the colour chosen for our classroom. ___

How many did you get right? ☐

Grammar

Participle clauses

There are two kinds of participles. The present participle (verb + -ing) and the past participle (verb + -ed or irregular form).

We can use participles in participle clauses to make sentences shorter. They can replace the subject and the verb in a sentence if the subject of both clauses is the same. We use a present participle if the verb is active and a past participle if the verb is passive.
Before **leaving** the house, Nathan locked all the windows.
Asked if he wanted to go out, Simon replied that he was too tired.

We can also use a participle to replace a relative pronoun and verb.
The boy **who was asked** to join the team was delighted.
The boy **asked** to join the team was delighted.
The girl **who wanted** to go home early pretended to be ill.
The girl **wanting** to go home early pretended to be ill.

Grammar Exercises

2 Circle the correct words.
1. I'd like to buy the jacket **displayed / displaying** in the window, please.
2. **Not been / Not being** able to find a taxi, we walked home.
3. The man **playing / who playing** the piano is my brother.
4. **Caught / Catching** shoplifting, the boy asked them to let him go.
5. All pupils **wanted / wanting** to go on the trip must pay before the end of the week.
6. **Knowing / Knew** the show would be popular, I bought my tickets early.
7. I hurt my arm **playing / played** volleyball.
8. **Beaten / Beating** by a better team again, we decided to take up a different sport.
9. The subjects **taught / teaching** in American schools are the same as here.
10. **Walked / Walking** through the park, I decided I need to change my life.

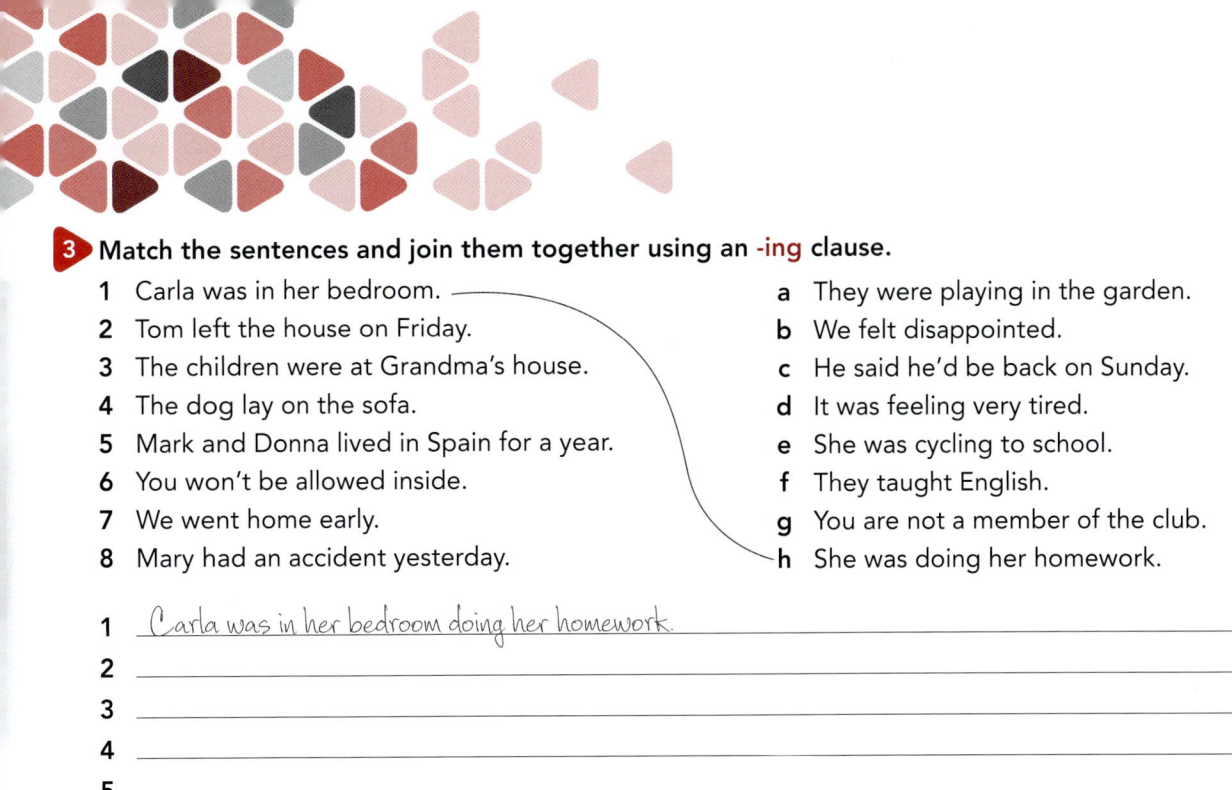

3 Match the sentences and join them together using an **-ing** clause.

1 Carla was in her bedroom.
2 Tom left the house on Friday.
3 The children were at Grandma's house.
4 The dog lay on the sofa.
5 Mark and Donna lived in Spain for a year.
6 You won't be allowed inside.
7 We went home early.
8 Mary had an accident yesterday.

a They were playing in the garden.
b We felt disappointed.
c He said he'd be back on Sunday.
d It was feeling very tired.
e She was cycling to school.
f They taught English.
g You are not a member of the club.
h She was doing her homework.

1 *Carla was in her bedroom doing her homework.*
2 _____
3 _____
4 _____
5 _____
6 _____
7 _____
8 _____

4 Rewrite the sentences using a present participle clause.

1 Because I wanted to meet Teri, I went to the train station.

2 We didn't know the city, so we bought a map.

3 I thought you'd like this, so I bought it for you.

4 She isn't from this country, so she needs to show her passport.

5 I went to bed early because I did not feel well.

6 While she was sitting on her bed, she had a brilliant idea.

5 Rewrite the sentences using a past participle clause.

1 The man was found not guilty and he started to laugh.
   Found not guilty, the man started to laugh.
2 The teacher didn't know what to say when she was asked a grammar question.

3 The woman who was sentenced to five years in prison will get out in 2018.

4 When he was injured, the boy was taken to hospital.

5 Everyone loved Emily, but she was very shy.

6 English is an important language to learn because it is spoken all over the world.

Unit 22

6 Complete the sentences with the correct form of these verbs.

bark   break   call   frighten   live   offer   study   work

1 The kids were woken up by a dog _____.
2 _____ in a flat, we decided not to get any pets.
3 Anybody _____ French at our school can go on the trip to Paris.
4 The window _____ by my sister has now been replaced.
5 _____ a job in a music shop, I was very happy.
6 A girl _____ Simone sent you a text message.
7 The man _____ at the petrol station was very rude.
8 _____ by the thunderstorm, our cat hid under the sofa.

7 Find the mistakes and correct the sentences. They should have participle clauses.

1 Not know her phone number, I sent her an email.
_____
2 Delighting to be invited to the party, I accepted.
_____
3 The woman who singing on the stage is my mum.
_____
4 Who are those people stood outside the police station?
_____
5 The man that arrested was questioned by the police for five hours.
_____
6 I was unable to sleep because of the wind blowed outside.
_____
7 Think the children might be thirsty, I made some lemonade.
_____
8 Sonia was at the swimming pool, she practising for the competition.
_____

Vocabulary

Prepositions

8 Complete the phrases with these prepositions. You will need to use some prepositions more than once.

for   through   to   with

1 to be familiar   _____
2 to vote   _____
3 to be similar   _____
4 to pay attention _____
5 to rush   _____
6 to be responsible _____
7 to be halfway   _____
8 to work   _____

9 Complete the sentences with the correct form of the phrases from 8.

1 You need to _____ your partner to complete this exercise.
2 This story is quite _____ the one you read to us last week.
3 Who is _____ breaking this plate?
4 Are you _____ the novels of J.K. Rowling?
5 I was _____ the book when I decided to give up – it was so boring!
6 It's hard to _____ what you are saying with this loud music playing.
7 She _____ her last task so that she could go home early.
8 Who did you _____ in the last election?

Exam Practice

10 Complete the second sentence so that it has a similar meaning to the first sentence, using the word given. Do not change the word given. You must use between two and five words.

1 I didn't understand the word, so I looked it up in the dictionary.
understanding
Not _____, I looked it up in the dictionary.

2 Not being hungry, the children left the table.
because
The children left the table _____ hungry.

3 The lessons that Mr Brown teaches have been cancelled.
taught
The lessons _____ have been cancelled.

4 Hurt by the accusations, Maryam didn't go outside for a month.
who
Maryam, _____ the accusations, didn't go outside for a month.

5 Do you know the rules of chess?
familiar
Are _____ the rules of chess?

6 Who is in charge of collecting donations?
responsible
Who _____ collecting donations?

7 My taste in music is almost the same as my sister's taste in music.
to
My sister's taste in music _____ mine.

8 Sometimes I find it hard to concentrate in class.
attention
Sometimes I find it hard _____ in class.

11 Use the word in capitals to form a word that fits in the gap.

1 _____ this was a kitchen, but we turned it into a dining room. **ORIGIN**
2 We have to pay a lot of _____ for this old car. **INSURE**
3 Do you have _____ to film in this building? **PERMIT**
4 Robin Hood is a _____ figure in English history. **LEGEND**
5 I'll wait for you at the _____ to the museum. **ENTER**
6 They arrested the _____ at his home last night. **ARSON**
7 We have a large _____ of tourist attractions in this city. **VARY**
8 Did you know that he had a _____ record? **CRIME**

Writing

12 Write four sentences in your notebook which are true for you. Use the structures shown in the examples.

Watching TV last night, I saw my teacher interviewed by a reporter.
Given the chance, I'd go on holiday to Brazil.
I haven't read any books written in French.
I never talk to people sitting next to me on public transport.

Unit 23

Awareness

1 Which of these sentences are correct (C) and incorrect (I)?

1. We have had the hall redecorated. ___
2. Have you have had your hearing tested? ___
3. What time are you have your car fixed? ___
4. She's having her nails manicured at the moment. ___
5. We got our house burgled last week. ___
6. Are you getting your suit cleaning for the party? ___
7. Have you ever had your computer checked for viruses? ___
8. I lost my certificate, but had got it replaced very quickly. ___
9. He will have his jeans washed by his mum. ___
10. How often do you getting your nails done? ___

How many did you get right? ☐

Grammar

Causative

We use the causative to
- say that someone has arranged for somebody to do something for them.
Most people **have** their eyes **tested** once a year.
- say that something unpleasant happened to someone.
I **had** my bike **stolen** last week.

We form the causative with *have* + object + past participle. It can be used in a variety of tenses. When we want to mention the agent, we use the word *by*.
We **have had** new carpets **fitted**.
My grandmother **used to have** her hair **styled** every week.
You **will have** your driving licence **checked by** a police officer.

Note

We can also use *get* + object + past participle. This structure is less formal. However, when we talk about unpleasant events, we must use *have*.
I **got** my computer **repaired** in the shop across the road.

Grammar Exercises

2 Circle the correct words.

1. Did you get the presents **wrap / wrapped** in the shop?
2. I'm **get / getting** my trousers shortened.
3. He **has had / had** his suit dry cleaned yesterday.
4. Are you going to **have / got** your homework checked?
5. It's a long time since we had our car **wash / washed**.
6. Jane **had / got** her finger broken playing basketball.
7. You must **get / to have** your teeth polished soon.
8. Where do you usually **have / got** your hair cut?

3 Complete the sentences using the causative form.

1. We _____ once since we bought it. (the swimming pool / fill)
2. They _____ when I visited them. (the garden / tidy)
3. I _____ (already / my bag / steal) by the time I checked in to the hotel.
4. He _____ at the moment. (his jeans / wash)
5. We _____ last week. (our front door / paint)
6. Ron _____ once a year. (his car / replace)

4 Rewrite the sentences using the causative form.

1 Someone stole her handbag.
She _____.

2 He's polishing my shoes.
I _____.

3 Someone broke into my uncle's car.
My uncle _____.

4 The baker is going to make a birthday cake for me tomorrow.
I'm _____.

5 A mechanic fixed Susan's car for her.
Susan _____.

6 A manicurist is trimming my toenails.
I'm _____.

7 Tomorrow, someone is going to design a website for me.
I _____.

8 Last month some photos were taken of us.
We _____.

5 Write answers to the questions.

1 Does she cut her own hair?
No, _she has it cut by her mum_____. (her mum)

2 Are you going to repair that computer?
No, _____. (at a computer shop)

3 Did you design this website yourself?
No, _____. (a web designer)

4 Will he fix his own bicycle?
No, _____. (at a bike shop)

5 Do you and your friend prepare your own meals?
No, _____. (by our mums)

6 Is she going to make her own clothes?
No, _____. (by a famous designer)

7 Does your dad service the car himself?
No, _____. (at a garage)

8 Will you examine your own teeth?
No, _____. (by a dentist)

6 Write questions for the answers.

1 _Who do you have your clothes designed by?_ I have my clothes designed by Mario.
2 _____ I'm going to get Sam to fix my bike.
3 _____ I had my feet massaged last week.
4 _____ I need to get my laptop fixed.
5 _____ I get my mum to do my maths homework.
6 _____ I have my eyes checked three times a year.
7 _____ I had my glasses made in Turkey.
8 _____ I had my phone installed six months ago.

Unit 23

7 Find the mistakes and correct the sentences.

1 Sammy got her mobile phone stolen last night.
2 Did you had your boots mended?
3 Mrs Jones is have her shopping delivered this evening.
4 We always have our Christmas presents wrap for us.
5 How often do you getting your hair styled?
6 I hope you will getting that jacket cleaned soon.
7 They had already had their luggage send to the wrong place.
8 We get the water in our pool tested at the moment.

Vocabulary

Phrasal verbs

8 Complete the phrasal verbs with these prepositions. You will need to use some of them more than once.

in   off   on   out   up

1 do _____ – to fasten with a zip or button
2 try _____ – to see if a piece of clothing looks nice or fits
3 wear _____ – to use something so much that it becomes useless
4 take _____ – to remove clothes from your body
5 dress _____ – to wear smart clothes
6 put _____ – to place clothes on your body and wear them
7 take _____ – to make a piece of clothing smaller and tighter
8 take _____ – to shorten a piece of clothing

9 Complete the sentences with the correct form of the phrasal verbs from 8.

1 Those trousers are too long. I'll have them _____.
2 Here, _____ this jumper – it's cold outside.
3 We _____ our boots when we came in from the fields.
4 You should _____ that jacket because it's very windy today.
5 It was such an expensive hotel that we had to _____ for dinner.
6 Sue has lost a lot of weight, and has had to have all her dresses _____.
7 Always _____ clothes before you buy them – they might not fit!
8 It doesn't take our postman long to _____ a pair of shoes because he walks miles every day.

Exam Practice

10 Complete the second sentence so that it has a similar meaning to the first sentence, using the word given. Do not change the word given. You must use between two and five words.

1. Somebody has already stolen three pens from me.
   had
   I've _____ from me.

2. A repair man came to fix our washing machine.
   got
   We _____ by a repair man.

3. This room needs tidying before the guests arrive.
   tidied
   We must _____ before the guests arrive.

4. Tom's dad always does his homework for him.
   gets
   Tom _____ for him by his dad.

5. Is someone going to collect your prize for you?
   have
   Are you _____ collected?

6. They'll send Sam his new stereo next week.
   delivered
   Sam will _____ next week.

7. Our beds were made for us every day on holiday.
   had
   We _____ for us every day on holiday.

8. They're going to build a new treehouse for us tomorrow.
   built
   Tomorrow we're going to _____ for us.

11 Choose the correct answers.

1. What time are you going to ___ your eyebrows trimmed?
   a have   b getting   c got   d had
2. They had all their children ___ how to play an instrument.
   a teach   b learnt   c taught   d teaching
3. I can't do ___ my jeans – they're too tight!
   a off   b up   c over   d out
4. Why don't you ___ this on and see if it fits you?
   a make   b have   c do   d try
5. You'll ___ out those shoes if you keep running every day.
   a push   b wear   c break   d dry
6. Take that hat ___ when you come into my house.
   a up   b out   c over   d off
7. If the dress is too long, I'll have it taken ___ by my aunt.
   a up   b out   c over   d down
8. You don't have to ___ up to eat here – it's not that formal.
   a make   b work   c wake   d dress

Writing

12 Imagine you have just become very rich. You do not have to do anything for yourself anymore. In your notebook, write six things that you now have done for you.

I have all my meals cooked for me by a celebrity chef.

Unit 24

Awareness

1 Which of these sentences are correct (C) and incorrect (I)?

1. Not only I do love to eat pizzas, but I also cook them! ___
2. It's time you have a bath. ___
3. Never have I heard such a stupid story. ___
4. Under no circumstances you can borrow my socks. ___
5. The time's high I bought some new clothes. ___
6. It's about time I taught you to dance. ___
7. Under no circumstances are you allowed to enter this room. ___
8. I've never been to such a boring lecture. ___
9. Not only is it very expensive, but it also is ugly. ___
10. It's time I went home. ___

How many did you get right? ☐

Grammar

Inversion: Under no circumstances, never & not only ... but also

We can use *under no circumstances*, *never* and *not only ... but also* at the beginning of a sentence for emphasis. When we do this, the word order changes. This is called inversion.
Steve has never seen a horror film.
Never has Steve seen a horror film.
Jake not only collects paintings, he sells them.
Not only does Jake collect paintings, **but** he **also** sells them.
You are not allowed to take photographs here under any circumstances.
Under no circumstances are you allowed to take photographs here.

It's (about/high) time

We can use *it's time*, *it's about time* and *it's high time* + past tense to talk about something that should have already been done in the present.
It's time you **stopped** leaving your clothes on the floor.
It's about time I **started** work on my project.
It's high time she **learnt** to ride a bicycle.

Grammar Exercises

2 Circle the correct words.

1. Never **had she / she had** eaten such delicious food.
2. Not only do I play football, **and / but** I also play tennis.
3. Under no circumstances **should you / you should** feed the animals.
4. It's time you **make / made** up your own mind.
5. Not only **designs he / does he design** his own software, he also teaches it.
6. Under no circumstances **are they allowed / they are allowed** to smoke.
7. It's about time Mandy **does / did** some work.
8. Never have I **seen / saw** such a beautiful sunset.

134

3 Combine the sentences using **Not only ... but also**.

1 We bought some new clothes. We also bought new shoes.

2 She likes to play volleyball. She's also a good footballer.

3 They had been staying at an expensive hotel. They had hired a Mercedes, too.

4 My cat is very ugly. It has a nasty personality, too.

5 The weather was very hot, and I was very thirsty.

6 This project is going to take a long time, and it's not going to be very useful.

7 We sell books and CDs too.

8 That film was both exciting and funny.

4 Invert the sentences.

1 Students may not, under any circumstances, use their mobile phones.
   Under no _____.

2 I've never wanted anything so much in my life.
   Never _____.

3 You're not allowed to park here under any circumstances.
   Under _____.

4 She had never met anyone so rich before.
   Never _____.

5 You rarely see telephone boxes these days.
   Rarely _____.

6 Children can not, under any circumstances, enter the sauna.
   Under no _____.

7 I've seldom regretted doing anything in my life.
   Seldom _____.

8 You should not tell Jenny about this under any circumstances.
   Under no _____.

5 Choose the correct answers.

1 ___ has my father been so angry.
   a Never
   b It's time
   c Not only

2 ___ you spoke to someone about your problem.
   a Rarely
   b Under no circumstances
   c It's time

3 ___ are animals allowed in the rooms.
   a It's high time
   b Not only
   c Under no circumstances

4 ___ did I suspect that Daniel was a burglar.
   a Not only
   b Never
   c Seldom

5 ___ was that a silly thing to do, it was also selfish.
   a Seldom
   b Not only
   c It's high time

6 ___ can we afford to eat in a restaurant.
   a Seldom
   b Not only
   c It's about time

Unit 24

6 Write sentences with **It's time ...** and one of these verbs.

> build   go   learn   leave   start   tell   wake up   wash

1 John can't tie his shoe laces.
   It's time he learnt.

2 Sarah hasn't been to the dentist's for three years.

3 Martin hasn't started his project yet.

4 Susan's car has been very dirty for months.

5 Greg still doesn't know about the party.

6 There's still no sports centre in my town.

7 It's late, but these people are still here.

8 It's one o'clock in the afternoon and David is still asleep.

7 Find the mistakes and correct the sentences.

1 Not only do I play the guitar, but also I sing.

2 Under no circumstances you're allowed to drive this car.

3 Never had she saw such an untidy room.

4 It's time we go.

5 I've never been the seaside before.

6 Not only is it cheap, it also is rather pretty.

7 It's time about for you to go to bed.

8 Under no circumstances should you spoke to the prisoners.

Vocabulary

Word formation

8 Match the words with their meanings.

1 accessory ☐   a to change
2 afford ☐   b a precious stone used to decorate the body
3 alternate ☐   c the quality of being beautiful and attractive
4 collect ☐   d to bring a group of things together
5 exclusive ☐   e not shared with another thing or person
6 fashion ☐   f something extra
7 glamour ☐   g to have enough money to pay for something
8 jewel ☐   h popular clothing styles

9 Use the word in capitals to form a word that fits in the gap.

1 You have a very nice _____ of shoes here.　　　　COLLECT
2 We sold our story _____ to one newspaper.　　　　EXCLUSIVE
3 That's a nice dress – now you need to _____ with a scarf.　　　　ACCESSORY
4 She always likes getting _____ as birthday presents.　　　　JEWEL
5 She looks really _____ in that white dress.　　　　GLAMOUR
6 My shoes are comfortable, but not _____.　　　　FASHION
7 Dan's sister has a very _____ way of dressing.　　　　ALTERNATE
8 I couldn't possibly buy that hat – it's completely _____ for me!　　　　AFFORD

Exam Practice

10 Complete the second sentence so that it has a similar meaning to the first sentence, using the word given. Do not change the word given. You must use between two and five words.

1 Penny hasn't tidied her room for months – she should.
   about
   It _____ her room.

2 You should never stroke a dog you do not know.
   circumstances
   Under _____ a dog you do not know.

3 Gerry is handsome and clever.
   only
   Not only _____, but he is also clever.

4 She had never been to a circus before.
   she
   Never _____ to a circus before.

5 You must never point a gun at anybody.
   should
   Under _____ a gun at anybody.

6 You really ought to start revising for your exams.
   high
   It's _____ revising for your exams.

7 I never want to go to that place again.
   do
   Never _____ go to that place again.

11 Complete the sentences with the word that best fits each gap.

1 It's about _____ you got up.
2 Under _____ circumstances should you press this button.
3 Never _____ I met such a beautiful woman.
4 Not _____ did she buy a new skirt, but she also bought a hat.
5 Seldom _____ we go out on Friday nights these days.
6 It's about time we _____ to the cinema.
7 Hardly ever have I _____ such terrible music.
8 Not only is he a poor singer, _____ he was also very rude to the audience.

Writing

12 Write four sentences in your notebook which are true for you. Use these structures:

- Never have I ...
- Not only ... but also ...
- Under no circumstances ...
- It's about time ...

Grammar

1 Join the sentences using a relative pronoun. Use defining or non-defining relative clauses.

1 Gina is a good footballer. Her dad used to play for Arsenal.

2 The concert was wonderful. Everybody was dancing there.

3 The bicycle has been sold. You wanted it.

4 They're closing the swimming pool. I used to go there every week.

5 Daniel is my best friend. His mother is the head teacher at my school.

6 Steve has a new car. He has always loved driving.

2 Rewrite the sentences with a present or past participle clause.

1 He doesn't have a driving licence, so he can't hire a car.

2 This film was made in the 1950s, but it's still exciting.

3 He was annoyed when the waiter asked him to change tables.

4 While she was riding home, she realised she had forgotten something.

5 Nobody liked Simon because he was very unfriendly.

6 These phones are very cheap and they're sold all over the world.

3 Complete the sentences using the causative form.

1 We _____ at the studio this afternoon. (our photo / take)
2 He _____ yet. (not / his car / service)
3 Did she _____ by a professional? (the website / design)
4 We _____ twice last year. (house / burgle)
5 Steve _____ yesterday. (his mobile / steal)
6 Do you _____ every time you enter a new country? (passport / stamp)
7 Will you _____ by tomorrow? (your computer / repair)
8 My friend _____ when I called on him. (his toenails / cut)

4 Choose the correct answers.

1 Not only ___ boring, but it's also very long.
   a this show is
   b is this show
   c this show was
2 Never ___ a cold drink so much!
   a I hadn't enjoyed
   b hadn't I enjoyed
   c had I enjoyed
3 It's high time you ___ to drive.
   a learnt
   b have learnt
   c did learn
4 Under no circumstances ___ this room.
   a you leave
   b you can leave
   c can you leave
5 Never ___ such a colourful dress.
   a have I seen
   b I have seen
   c I saw
6 Not only ___ a house in the country, but he also has a flat in the city.
   a has he
   b does he have
   c he does have
7 It's about time we ___ a holiday somewhere warm.
   a have had
   b had
   c have
8 Under no circumstances ___ the pool at night.
   a they should use
   b they shouldn't use
   c should they use

5 Circle the correct words.

1 My mum, **who / that** is a very good cook, has made a cake.
2 We found the children **sit / sitting** in the treehouse.
3 You should **get / to have** your eyes tested!
4 Never **had he / he had** worn such an expensive suit.
5 It's high time you **do / did** some work in this house.
6 Sam **had / got** his leg broken when he was ice-skating.
7 **Running / Ran** home after school, I met Charlie.
8 Early morning is the time **when / where** we take the dogs to the park.

6 Find the mistakes and correct the sentences.

1 Dad's university, where he studied there for four years, is in Manchester.
   _____
2 The pupil that chosen to represent the school is called Tonya.
   _____
3 I'm have my shoes polished in the morning.
   _____
4 Not only is this the prettiest, it also is the least expensive.
   _____
5 Thought it was going to rain, I took my umbrella with me.
   _____
6 We got our clothes stolen while we were swimming in the sea.
   _____
7 My uncle, that my mum doesn't like, is coming to stay with us.
   _____
8 It's time you go to school.
   _____

Review 6 139

Review 6

Exam Practice

7 For questions 1–12, read the text below and think of the word which best fits each gap. Use only one word in each gap. There is an example at the beginning (0).

The Ozone Layer

The ozone layer, (0) __which__ consists (1) _____ a thin band of ozone gas high above the earth's surface, is extremely important to life on our planet. (2) _____ is this thin layer of gas that protects life on earth from the harmful, ultra-violet light which comes from the sun.

Since the 1960s, scientists have observed 'holes' in the ozone layer and done research (3) _____ the phenomenon. The holes (4) _____ caused by chemicals called CFCs being released into the atmosphere. CFCs, which (5) _____ destroy huge amounts of ozone, enter the atmosphere when refrigerators are destroyed and when aerosol sprays are used.

The results of the damage which has been (6) _____ to the ozone layer have been known for a number of years. Ultra-violet light kills plant life, thus reducing (7) _____ amount of oxygen in the atmosphere. Also, skin cancer is becoming more common. Nowadays, fridges and sprays are not normally made with harmful CFCs in them, but, because (8) _____ are so many old fridges being thrown (9) _____ all the time, scientists have not been (10) _____ to stop the destruction.

If the prediction that most of the ozone layer (11) _____ have been destroyed in 50 years' time comes true, humans will wish they (12) _____ never heard of CFCs!

8 For questions 13–22, read the text below. Use the word given in capitals at the end of each line to form a word that fits in the gap in the same line. There is an example at the beginning (0).

The sound of music

Thanks to the latest (0) __developments__ in dairy farming, there is a new sound	DEVELOP
to be heard on the grassy slopes of (13) _____ Europe. Early in the	CENTRE
morning, (14) _____ of the sparsely populated agricultural regions	INHABIT
of Austria and Southern Germany wake up to (15) _____ melodies	ROMANCE
being played ... to cows! The effect of music on mood has been widely researched and	
documented. However, never has it been put to such (16) _____	PRACTICE
use as it has in this case. The farmers, who use both live and recorded music to calm the	
cattle, are keen to make the lives of their animals as calm and (17) _____	PEACE
as possible. They claim that the music (18) _____ up the animals'	BRIGHT
day by allowing them to relax. Not only does this (19) _____ increase	SUBSTANCE
the amount of milk produced, but it also helps the cows give it up much more easily.	
To their (20) _____, farmers have also found that the quality of milk	ASTONISH
is better. With such (21) _____ results, it's not surprising that	REMARK
agriculturalists are now broadening the scope of their experiments. Plans are currently	
being made to see how (22) _____ music is in getting other farm	EFFECT
animals to become more productive.	

140

Grammar

9 For questions 1–10, choose the word or phrase that best completes the sentence or conversation.

1 Never ___ such an interesting explanation of the causative!
   A I have heard
   B I had heard
   C have I heard
   D had I heard

2 'Nice hair. Did you cut it yourself?'
   'No, I ___ by my eleven-year-old nephew.'
   A cut it
   B got it
   C had it cut
   D it had cut

3 The girl ___ is my cousin.
   A singing
   B who sing
   C who singing
   D sings

4 'Did you have a good holiday?'
   'No. The hotel ___ was terrible.'
   A we stayed
   B where we stayed
   C that we stayed
   D we were staying

5 It's ___ your homework!
   A about time did you
   B high did you time
   C high time you did
   D time about you did

6 'My computer still isn't working.'
   'I thought you ___ last week.'
   A were fixed
   B had fixed
   C it had fixed
   D had it fixed

7 'What's the matter?'
   'I hurt my leg ___ basketball.'
   A to play
   B played
   C playing
   D play

8 They're destroying the library ___.
   A I used to study
   B that I used to study
   C I used to study there
   D where I used to study

9 ___ to see the stage, we left the theatre.
   A Not being able
   B Being not able
   C Able not
   D Not been able

10 Under no circumstances ___ during the test.
   A you allowed to talk
   B are you allowed to talk
   C you are allowed to talk
   D allowed are you to talk

Vocabulary

10 For questions 11–20, choose the word or phrase that best completes the sentence.

11 I hope the thief is ___ arrest by now.
   A under
   B over
   C in
   D with

12 You should ___ up your coat – it's cold!
   A make
   B put
   C tie
   D do

13 He ___ not guilty to the charge, but I know he did it.
   A told
   B pleaded
   C begged
   D prayed

14 I'm not familiar ___ the rules of this game.
   A in
   B on
   C with
   D to

15 I can't believe they let that arsonist ___ with a fine.
   A off
   B away
   C out
   D from

16 You had better mend your ___ or you'll get into big trouble one day.
   A paths
   B roads
   C acts
   D ways

17 ___ off your boots before you come in, please.
   A Show
   B Take
   C Send
   D Put

18 If you ___ the law, you'll be arrested.
   A break
   B hurt
   C snap
   D damage

19 I gave up on the book when I was halfway ___ it – it was so boring!
   A in
   B over
   C through
   D past

20 They have played that CD so much it's almost worn ___.
   A out
   B on
   C off
   D over

Review 6 141

Irregular Verbs

Infinitive	Past Simple	Past Participle
be	was/were	been
beat	beat	beaten
become	became	become
begin	began	begun
bite	bit	bitten
blow	blew	blown
break	broke	broken
bring	brought	brought
broadcast	broadcast	broadcast
build	built	built
burn	burnt	burnt
buy	bought	bought
can	could	–
catch	caught	caught
choose	chose	chosen
come	came	come
cost	cost	cost
cut	cut	cut
deal	dealt	dealt
dig	dug	dug
do	did	done
draw	drew	drawn
dream	dreamt	dreamt
drink	drank	drunk
drive	drove	driven
eat	ate	eaten
fall	fell	fallen
feed	fed	fed
feel	felt	felt
fight	fought	fought
find	found	found
fly	flew	flown
forecast	forecast	forecast
forget	forgot	forgotten
get	got	got
give	gave	given
go	went	gone
grow	grew	grown
hang	hung	hung
have	had	had
hear	heard	heard
hide	hid	hidden
hit	hit	hit
hold	held	held
hurt	hurt	hurt
keep	kept	kept
know	knew	known
lead	led	led
learn	learnt	learnt
leave	left	left
lend	lent	lent
let	let	let
lie	lay	lain

Infinitive	Past Simple	Past Participle
light	lit	lit
lose	lost	lost
may	might	–
mean	meant	meant
make	made	made
meet	met	met
pay	paid	paid
prove	proved	proven
put	put	put
read	read [red]	read [red]
ride	rode	ridden
ring	rang	rung
rise	rose	risen
run	ran	run
say	said	said
see	saw	seen
sell	sold	sold
send	sent	sent
set	set	set
shake	shook	shaken
shine	shone	shone
show	showed	shown
shoot	shot	shot
shut	shut	shut
sing	sang	sung
sink	sank	sunk
sit	sat	sat
sleep	slept	slept
slide	slid	slid
smell	smelt	smelt
speak	spoke	spoken
speed	sped	sped
spend	spent	spent
spread	spread	spread
stand	stood	stood
steal	stole	stolen
stick	stuck	stuck
stink	stank	stunk
sweep	swept	swept
swim	swam	swum
take	took	taken
teach	taught	taught
tell	told	told
think	thought	thought
throw	threw	thrown
understand	understood	understood
wake	woke	woken
wear	wore	worn
win	won	won
write	wrote	written
win	won	won
write	wrote	written

Phrasal verbs

back out	= to decide not to do something you had arranged to do	(U8)
back up to	= to save a copy of your work	(U8)
believe in	= to think that something exists	(U3)
blast off	= (of a rocket) to leave the earth and head for space	(U8)
bring out	= to publish	(U15)
bring round	= to convince someone that your point of view is correct	(U15)
check in	= to arrive at a hotel	(U20)
come up with	= to think of and create something new	(U8)
die out	= to become extinct or disappear	(U11)
dig up	= to remove something from the ground	(U11)
do up	= to fasten with a zip or button	(U23)
dress up	= to wear smart clothes	(U23)
drop off	= to take someone somewhere and leave them	(U20)
get around	= to move from place to place	(U20)
get away	= to escape	(U20)
get on	= to board a plane, train	(U20)
hook up	= to connect to a power supply	(U8)
let out	= to make a certain sound	(U3)
log in	= to gain access to a computer	(U8)
look into	= to examine or study something	(U3)
make out	= to manage to see something which is difficult to see	(U3)
make up	= to say something that isn't true	(U3)
pick out	= to choose	(U15)
pick up	= to collect someone or something and take them somewhere	(U15)
put off	= to discourage	(U11)
put on	= to place clothes on your body and wear them	(U23)
put up	= to assemble or build something	(U20)
put up with	= to tolerate something unpleasant	(U11)
ring back	= to return a phone call	(U15)
ring in	= to phone a TV or radio station	(U15)
see off	= to wave goodbye to someone leaving from an airport, station	(U20)
set off	= to begin a journey / to leave on a journey	(U8, U11)
set out	= to begin a journey	(U20)
set up	= to prepare or organise / to prepare something for use	(U8, U11)
stick to	= to remain on the same topic	(U3)
take in	= to make a piece of clothing smaller and tighter	(U23)
take in	= to trick or deceive somebody	(U3)
take off	= to become quickly successful	(U11)
take off	= to remove clothes from your body	(U23)
take over	= to start to have control of something	(U11)
take place	= to happen	(U3)
take up	= to shorten a piece of clothing	(U23)
try on	= to see if a piece of clothing looks nice or fits	(U23)
tune in	= to choose a particular radio station	(U15)
tune out	= to stop paying attention to something	(U15)
wear out	= to use something so much that it becomes useless	(U23)

Prepositions

according **to**	(U9)	find a solution **to**	(U18)
arrive/be **on** time	(U18)	focus **on**	(U5)
at risk **of**	(U5)	hold something **by**	(U14)
(be) a member **of**	(U5)	**in** my opinion	(U18)
(be) banned **from**	(U9)	live **on**	(U14)
(be) different **from**	(U9, U14)	live to be **over**	(U5)
(be) familiar **with**	(U22)	make a success **of**	(U9)
(be) good **at**	(U9)	**on** behalf of	(U18)
(be) halfway **through**	(U22)	pay attention **to**	(U22)
(be) **in** debt	(U18)	prevent **from**	(U14)
(be) out **of** work	(U18)	reach the top **of**	(U18)
(be) responsible **for**	(U22)	react **to** something	(U18)
(be) similar **to**	(U22)	recover **from**	(U14)
(be) surprised **at**	(U9)	rush **through**	(U22)
(be) surprised **by**	(U14)	spread **to**	(U9)
(be) vaccinated **against**	(U5)	vote **for**	(U22)
contribute **to**	(U5)	work **on**	(U5)
depend **on**	(U5)	work **with**	(U22)
do research **on**	(U14)		
dream **of**	(U9)		
drop **by**	(U14)		

145

Collocations & Expressions

a ray of sunshine	(U13)	have confidence in	(U2)
accept responsibility for (something)	(U21)	have your head in the clouds	(U13)
as fast as lightning	(U13)	keep in touch	(U1)
(be) associated with	(U2)	keep your promise	(U1)
(be) back on your feet	(U6)	launch a product	(U17)
(be) engaged to	(U2)	lay off	(U17)
(be) in charge	(U17)	let (somebody) off	(U21)
(be) in deep water	(U13)	make a difference	(U1)
(be) involved with	(U2)	make a profit	(U10)
(be) on your last legs	(U6)	make progress	(U10)
(be) under arrest	(U21)	make trouble	(U1)
break a habit	(U1)	mend (your) ways	(U21)
break the ice	(U1)	pick (someone's) brains	(U6)
break the law	(U21)	plead (not) guilty	(U21)
do business	(U10)	recharge (your) batteries	(U6)
do (you) the world of good	(U6)	reject an offer	(U17)
do (your) best	(U10)	rely on	(U2)
feel fresh as a daisy	(U6)	save time	(U1)
feel under the weather	(U6, U13)	save your strength	(U1)
get the sack	(U17)	shout at	(U2)
go bankrupt	(U10)	solve the case	(U21)
go down a storm	(U13)	take chances	(U10)
go into partnership	(U10)	take on staff	(U17)
hand in your notice	(U17)	take your place	(U10)
have a frog in your throat	(U6)	throw caution to the wind	(U13)
have a police record	(U21)	work shifts	(U17)
have an effect on	(U2)		

Word formation

Adjective → Noun

CONFIDENT	CONFIDENCE	U2
CURIOUS	CURIOSITY	U8, U17
DIFFICULT	DIFFICULTY	R2
FOREIGN	FOREIGNER	U1
ILL	ILLNESS	U5
INTENSE	INTENSITY	U14
JEALOUS	JEALOUSY	U2
MODEST	MODESTY	U9
SIMILAR	SIMILARITY	U4
STABLE	STABILITY	U1

Adjective → Opposite adjective

CREDIBLE	INCREDIBLE	U8, U17
USUAL	UNUSUAL	U4, U9, U16

Adjective → Verb

BRIGHT	BRIGHTEN	R6
SOCIAL	SOCIALISE	U5
WEAK	WEAKEN	U3

Adverbs

ACCIDENT	ACCIDENTALLY	U5
BASIC	BASICALLY	U17
CARE	CAREFULLY	R3
CHEER	CHEERFULLY	U2
DRAMATIC	DRAMATICALLY	U20
EXCLUSIVE	EXCLUSIVELY	U24
FORTUNATE	UNFORTUNATELY	U14
GENERAL	GENERALLY	R2
NATURE	NATURALLY	U2, U20
ORIGIN	ORIGINALLY	U22
RISK	RISKY	U16
SUBSTANCE	SUBSTANTIALLY	R6
SUCCESS	SUCCESSFULLY	U9
THEORY	THEORETICALLY	U12

Noun → Adjective

ADVENTURE	ADVENTUROUS	U16
CATASTROPHE	CATASTROPHIC	U14
CENTRE	CENTRAL	R6
COLOUR	COLOURFUL	U20
ECONOMY	ECONOMIC	R5, R2
FASHION	FASHIONABLE	U24
GENE	GENETIC	U5
GLAMOUR	GLAMOROUS	U24
GYMNAST	GYMNASTIC	U2
INDUSTRY	INDUSTRIAL	U7
INFLUENCE	INFLUENTIAL	U9
LEGEND	LEGENDARY	U3, U22
LIFE	LIVING	R2
MARVEL	MARVELOUS	U8
MASS	MASSIVE	U14
MISERY	MISERABLE	R3
MOUNTAIN	MOUNTAINOUS	U19
MYSTERY	MYSTERIOUS	U3
MYTH	MYTHICAL	U14
NATION	NATIONAL	R5
OPTIMIST	OPTIMISTIC	U8, U9
PASSION	PASSIONATE	U17
PEACE	PEACEFUL	U1
PERSON	PERSONAL	R5
PRACTICE	PRACTICAL	R6
PSYCHOLOGY	PSYCHOLOGICAL	R5
RESIST	RESISTANT	U14
RIDICULE	RIDICULOUS	U4
ROMANCE	ROMANTIC	R6
TERROR	TERRIFYING	R2
THOUGHT	THOUGHTFUL	U1
VOLUNTEER	VOLUNTARY	R3
WEALTH	WEALTHY	U9
WEIGHT	WEIGHTLESS	U8

Noun → Noun

AGENT	AGENCY	U19
ARCHAEOLOGY	ARCHAEOLOGIST	U3
ARCHITECT	ARCHITECTURE	U19
ARSON	ARSONIST	U22
BREATH	BREATHING	R5
CHAMPION	CHAMPIONSHIP	U2
COMEDY	COMEDIAN	U12
CRIME	CRIMINAL	U22
DIET	DIETICIAN	U5
EFFECT	EFFECTIVE	R6
FRIEND	FRIENDSHIP	R3
JEWEL	JEWELLERY	U24
JOURNAL	JOURNALIST	U16
PERSON	PERSONALITY	U1
PHOTO	PHOTOGRAPHY	U16
POLITICS	POLITICIAN	U16
SCENE	SCENERY	U20

147

Word formation

Noun → Verb		
ACCESSORY	ACCESSORISE	U24
POWER	EMPOWER	U7
PROOF	PROVE	U12
EXAM	EXAMINE	U5
REVOLUTION	REVOLUTIONISE	U7

Prefixes		
AFFORD	UNAFFORDABLE	U24
APPEAR	DISAPPEARANCE	U3
AVOID	UNAVOIDABLE	R2
CONTINUE	DISCONTINUE	R3
COURAGE	ENCOURAGE	U8
EFFECT	INEFFECTIVE	R5
POPULATE	OVERPOPULATED	U3
SATISFY	UNSATISFYING	U16
SUCCESS	UNSUCCESSFUL	U17

Verb → Adjective		
ALTERNATE	ALTERNATIVE	U24
ATTRACT	ATTRACTIVE	U1
BOARD	BOARDING	U19
DESTROY	DESTRUCTIVE	U14
EXCEL	EXCELLENT	U7, U17
HOPE	HOPELESS	R3
IMPRESS	IMPRESSIVE	U20
INSPIRE	INSPIRATIONAL/INSPIRING	U7
REMARK	REMARKABLE	U4
REPEAT	REPETITIVE	U12
SATISFY	SATISFACTORY/SATISFYING	U12
STICK	STICKY	U4
SUSPECT	SUSPICIOUS	U2
TREAT	TREATABLE	U9
TRUST	TRUSTWORTHY	U1

Verb → Noun		
ACCOMMODATE	ACCOMMODATION	U19
ACT	ACTION	U16
ANALYSE	ANALYSIS	U12
ASSIGN	ASSIGNMENT	U17
ASTONISH	ASTONISHMENT	R6
BLIND	BLINDNESS	U9
COLLECT	COLLECTION	U24
COMBINE	COMBINATION	U17
CONCLUDE	CONCLUSION	U4
CONSUME	CONSUMPTION	U5
DEPART	DEPARTURE	U19
DEPRESS	DEPRESSION	U1
DETERMINE	DETERMINATION	R3
DEVELOP	DEVELOPMENT	U8
DISCOVER	DISCOVERY	U4, U12
DONATE	DONATION	R5
EDUCATE	EDUCATION	U2
ENTER	ENTRANCE	U22
EQUIP	EQUIPMENT	U20
ERUPT	ERUPTION	U14
EXPLAIN	EXPLANATION	U4
EXPLODE	EXPLOSION	U7
FAIL	FAILURE	R2
IMAGINE	IMAGINATION	U7
INHABIT	INHABITANT	R6
INSPIRE	INSPIRATION	R5
INSURE	INSURANCE	U22
INVESTIGATE	INVESTIGATION	U3
KNOW	KNOWLEDGE	U12, R3
LAND	LANDING	U19
OBLIGE	OBLIGATION	R5
PERMIT	PERMISSION	U22
POPULATE	POPULATION	U20
PRESS	PRESSURE	U5
REACT	REACTION	U7
RECOVER	RECOVERY	R3
REPRESENT	REPRESENTATIVE	R5
RESEARCH	RESEARCHER	U8
RESIDE	RESIDENT	U4
SETTLE	SETTLEMENT	U3
SITUATE	SITUATION	U4
SOLVE	SOLUTION	R2
TOUR	TOURIST	U19
TRAVEL	TRAVELLER	U20
VARY	VARIETY	U22

Close-Up B1+ English in Use Student's Book

Philip James

Publisher: Gavin McLean
Director of Content Development: Sarah Bideleux
Editorial Assistant: Sarah-Jane Platt
Project Editor: Amy Borthwick
Manufacturing Buyer: Elaine Willis
Art Director: Natasa Arsenidou
Cover Designer: Tania Diakaki
Compositor: Sofia Fourtouni

Acknowledgements

Editorial and project management by hyphen SA

© 2013 National Geographic Learning, a part of Cengage Learning

ALL RIGHTS RESERVED. No part of this work covered by the copyright herein may be reproduced, transmitted, stored or used in any form or by any means graphic, electronic, or mechanical, including but not limited to photocopying, recording, scanning, digitalising, taping, Web distribution, information networks, or information storage and retrieval systems, except as permitted under Section 107 or 108 of the 1976 United States Copyright Act, or applicable copyright law of another jurisdiction, without the prior written permission of the publisher.

> For permission to use material from this text or product, submit all requests online at **cengage.com/permissions**
>
> Further permissions questions can be emailed to **permissionrequest@cengage.com**.

ISBN: 978-1-4080-6164-0

National Geographic Learning
Cheriton House, North Way, Andover, Hampshire, SP10 5BE
United Kingdom

Cengage Learning is a leading provider of customised learning solutions with office locations around the globe, including Singapore, the United Kingdom, Australia, Mexico, Brazil and Japan.

Cengage Learning products are represented in Canada by Nelson Education Ltd.

Visit National Geographic Learning online at **ngl.cengage.com**
Visit our corporate website at **www.cengage.com**

Photo credits

Cover image: Shutterstock

All other images: Shutterstock

Printed in China by RR Donnelley
Print Number: 12 Print Year: 2020